Expelled

Expelled

JAMES LAWSON JR.
AND
VANDERBILT UNIVERSITY

BENJAMIN HOUSTON

VANDERBILT UNIVERSITY PRESS
Nashville, Tennessee

First printing 2026.

Library of Congress Cataloging-in-Publication Data on file

Names: Houston, Benjamin author
Title: Expelled : James Lawson Jr. and Vanderbilt University / Benjamin Houston.
Description: Nashville, Tennessee : Vanderbilt University Press, [2026] | Includes bibliographical references.
Identifiers: LCCN 2025047037 (print) | LCCN 2025047038 (ebook) | ISBN 9780826500120 paperback | ISBN 9780826500137 epub | ISBN 9780826500144 pdf
Subjects: LCSH: Vanderbilt University. Divinity School--Students--History--20th century | Lawson, James M., 1928-2024 | Civil rights workers--Tennessee--Nashville--History--20th century | Civil rights demonstrations--Tennessee--Nashville--History--20th century | Civil rights movements--Tennessee--Nashville--History--20th century
Classification: LCC E185.97.L38 H68 2026 (print) | LCC E185.97.L38 (ebook)
LC record available at https://lccn.loc.gov/2025047037
LC ebook record available at https://lccn.loc.gov/2025047038

Cover image courtesy of the James Lawson archive, Vanderbilt University.

CONTENTS

James Lawson Jr., Vanderbilt University student and Fellowship of Reconciliation activist. *Nashville Banner* Archives, Special Collections Division, Nashville Public Library

Introduction

AN UNCOMMON MAN tried to change Nashville. In doing so, he also decisively altered the trajectory of the civil rights movement. James Lawson, Methodist pastor and nonviolent activist, told a story many times about how he found his calling and knew what his life would be about. As a young person in Massillon, Ohio, he remembered telling his parents that he had slapped a white neighbor child who had called him a racist slur. The resultant conversations burrowed into his soul. In recounting the parenting that ensued: "my dad's position was that we had to defend ourselves"—perhaps no surprise, given his father's constant accessory of a .38 pistol. But his mother's stance differed: "No, Jacob, they can do it another way." Lawson recalled the "long soliloquy" that followed, tracing "who we were, what we were about as a family, and about our worship of God, and our participation at the St. James AME Zion congregation, and our religion, and Jesus—that meant we could not be injured by this misbehavior, of being called something racist." And her summative point was "there must be a better way."

He later said that "In a very real way, my life stood still. I realized in that stillness that I had changed forever." At once deeply personal but also educational, Lawson recounted this story frequently as a rhetorical touchstone for how he built an unparalleled career of nonviolent activism and instructed thousands in the same. What he shared less often was the visceral reaction to this conversation. The moment, he later put, was "a numinous experience" for him,

> because I heard a voice, which came from what, it seemed to me, a deep place in space, and then gradually I felt that it was coming from inside

> me, but from outside me, but it was coming to me and it was a voice deep within. That voice said, "Number one, you will never again fight anybody physically." And then secondly, as she was talking, I heard the same voice saying, "and you will find the better way."

It was, as he put it, the start of a journey, "and maybe that journey never ends."[1]

That journey brought him to Nashville. It is not hackneyed to understand his time there as an instance where one man shaped a particular historical moment profoundly. Lawson played an "incomparable" role in shaping Nashville's singular place in civil rights history. He moved there already well-established as an activist, deeply interlinked with networks of people trying to instill nonviolence more widely in Black communities across America. In doing that same work in Nashville, he cultivated a small cadre of ministers and students from the city's Black churches and universities. Under Lawson's tutelage, these regular people decided to do something extraordinary. They consciously chose to embrace bodily harm so as to literally step and sit outside the normal patterns of racism that intruded upon their lives.[2]

Helped by Lawson's preparatory work, these students were ready to act in 1960 when sit-ins shook the South in protest against the prevailing lunch-counter discrimination common to the era. Nashville's demonstrations were distinguished for exhibiting on a substantial scale an unusually disciplined and sophisticated form of nonviolent resistance. This sustained commitment eventually made Nashville the first major Southern city to desegregate its lunch counters. Equally importantly, many of those forged with nonviolent steel by Lawson during the Nashville campaign—famed activists like John Lewis, Diane Nash, Bernard Lafayette, and more—played critical roles in the subsequent Black Freedom Struggle. A strong Nashville contingent remained instrumental to forming and guiding the early years of the Student Nonviolent Coordinating Committee (SNCC), rescuing the Freedom Rides in 1961, and taking the Movement further into the heart of the segregationist South well into the 1960s. The story of nonviolence and lunch counters in Nashville, plus the formidable personalities who emerged from that struggle, drew a spotlight to the city even then. That vivid legacy has not dimmed today.[3]

We amplify and enrich that legacy by pausing to examine Lawson's stint in Nashville more closely. Indeed, the import of those years is only enhanced when we grapple with what Lawson endured and provoked at the time. His "time of testing" tells us much about the slow and uneven paths to justice for himself, and even more slowly for Nashville and the South.

This book centers on a few months in spring 1960 when Vanderbilt University expelled James Lawson because of the local lunch-counter demonstrations. As one person, "in a soft, sad voice," summarized it at the time, "A person and an event came to symbolize a very great set of principles—freedom of action, freedom of conscience, the nature of a university, and in this case the struggle of the Negro for rights." Typical accounts tracing Lawson's career or treating Nashville's civil rights history usually contain a paragraph or page about this expulsion. Lawson emerged as a featured target for segregationist rage even as the city still reeled from the protests. His ouster occurred while the sit-in campaign remained ongoing and during Lawson's final semester before graduating from Vanderbilt's Divinity School. A groundswell of outcries from white academic and religious circles as well as the wider Movement empowered some of Lawson's professors to support him publicly, eventually by resigning from the university.[4]

Lawson's expulsion was of course not the only civil rights-related persecution of this era. Indeed, it was not even the only one in Nashville. Yet the extent to which this crisis poisoned Vanderbilt's reputation cannot be underestimated. On campus, the episode exposed divided opinions across the university. Off campus, segregationists and white liberals fought over the case's implications. Ongoing media interest in both made headlines internationally. One person involved described it as "turmoil for a year" and added that "the aftereffects lasted a long time." The fallout, historian Paul Conkin commented, made Vanderbilt "one of the most widely reviled universities in the country."[5]

Given this tumult, there is much to unpack. Scholar Melissa Kean correctly understood the Lawson case as "byzantine in its complexity and important enough to warrant book-length treatment." Overviews of this episode tend to isolate certain issues implicit in the controversy rather than the full range and rarely explore precisely how those issues resonated with those implicated. And so this book tries to unpeel the many layers not fully depicted by those brief treatments. At once, the Lawson Affair encompassed issues about university governance, civil rights activism, and religious witness (both in formal academic arenas and as lived by Black activists). Embedded in those issues were further themes about the fraught intersections between moral codes and legal statutes, the role of nonviolent direct action in highlighting those intersections, and the public portrayal of a civil rights cause célèbre set against more complex realities. Put another way, this small sliver of Lawson's life story is actually an important account of a Black person's demand for equality in an elite white space and anticipates an even longer history. The ensuing power struggles over supporting or censoring Lawson led to uncertain ramifications about the relationship between individuals and the institutions. These questions factored into far broader debates about student activism, academic freedom, higher education, racial integration, the legal and moral ethics of civil disobedience, and more—issues that dominated well into the 1960s and indeed into today.[6]

As such, this book is a fuller and rounder account compared to previous treatments of the Lawson Affair. It draws from new sources: archival materials only recently made accessible, reflective accounts written by participants, and oral histories recalling the crisis. This evidence helps uncover extensive minutiae of a historical moment in granular detail—things like administrative memoranda, quiet consultations and corridor conversations, newspaper reports read one way by insiders and another by outsiders, phone calls between power-brokers where we can only surmise what was said, and more.

Such material is not always associated with the power and drama of the civil rights movement. But, for this story, such microcosmic details are essential. This account is richer precisely because the forensic intricacies help recalibrate a more comprehensive discerning. Here, the details matter. They matter for understanding Vanderbilt (and, by extension, organizations and institutions dealing with internal dissent). They matter in terms of understanding Nashville's racial history, a story often told too glibly, and the limits of that social evolution. They matter because they show that what happened was James Lawson's story, a narrative that he tried to control, and yet also a series of false and compounding narratives that usually remained outside of his grasp. And the details matter because they facilitate a more sophisticated understanding of people processing events in real time and filtered by their own perspectives. Those perceptions, and how they influenced events, betrayed a range of complex and contradictory responses. In that sense, this example is widely applicable to how people dealt with racial change in the moment during the civil rights era.

Lawson's expulsion generated power struggles, spiritual witness, political tussles, media misrepresentations, activism across a wide spectrum of commitment and belief, and more. It provoked among the protagonists a range of prejudicial acts, arrogant egoism, heroic stances, ambivalent feelings, and regrets. It broke friendships, tainted legacies, exposed tragic flaws, and hardened mentalities. One person suggested at the time that the Lawson case was worthy of a novel by famed author and Vanderbilt alumnus Robert Penn Warren—it had everything a good story needed except a sex angle. It is not necessarily a grand history. Indeed, it was a mere blip in the full sweep of James Lawson's journey dedicated to a life of social justice. But it is nonetheless an incredibly indicative one. This story underlines how patchily people and institutions absorbed the lessons that the civil rights movement tried to demonstrate.[7]

1
The Call to Nashville

JAMES LAWSON'S NONVIOLENT ETHOS was strengthened in very particular crucibles. His Methodist upbringing, specific parental influences, and a very intentional choice of experiences all shaped his beliefs. Although born in Uniontown, Pennsylvania, he was raised mostly in Massillon. Before moving to those places, Reverend James M. Lawson Senior's ministries spanned the Deep South, New England, and Midwest. In each locale, he actively supported or started local Urban League or NAACP chapters. His wife, Philane May Cover, Jamaican by birth, impressed the ethic of nonviolence upon the younger Lawson at an early age. Ignore the emptiness of racist words, she said. What mattered was love. As scholars note, these two poles of influence, seemingly paradoxical, actually complemented each other powerfully. His father's fierceness in confronting injustice directly found an especially vibrant expression through his mother's nonviolent stance. In this way, Lawson's career exemplified the notion that, despite the misguided stereotype of passive or weak resistance, nonviolence could be an intensely militant form of activism embodying values in the flesh.[1]

These two dispositions represented by his parents fused together in him early on, prompting his exploration of being religiously called and nonviolently rooted. He was active in Methodist youth networks from early in his teens. He staged a lunch counter sit-in with a friend in high school. He quit a workplace entirely after management replaced him with an inexperienced white boy and downgraded Lawson's job. His college years at Baldwin-Wallace University in Berea, Ohio, allowed him to actively study all the theological and philosophical underpinnings of nonviolence from diverse vantages. There, he also tested local barbers' willingness to cut Black hair and rebuffed an academic who scolded him for dating a white girl. In discussing this last incident, he later articulated a specific value central to his being: a "commitment that I'm not going to act unlike what I think I want to act like, or feel like acting. I'm not going to be disciplined, contorted into something that I'm not." He absolutely refused to carry himself differently even in segregated spaces. Altering or adjusting his behavior based on other people's expectations about Blackness only defiled his inner self while reinforcing misguided white beliefs. That sense of composure made him a "marked man" at Vanderbilt in 1960.[2]

Lawson deepened his commitment to nonviolence after college. In 1951, he opted against following protocols for an academic or religious exemption from Korean War service. His choice to be a conscientious objector, he felt, required him morally to profess that belief, regardless of the consequences, rather than merely avoid service with deferments. Consequently, he was sentenced to prison for three years, although his parole terms allowed him to become a Methodist missionary in Nagpur, India, and engage with Gandhian ideas closer to the source. There he heard news of the Montgomery Bus Boycott and knew that his trajectory would circle back to the Black Freedom Struggle in America. In planning this pivot, Lawson initially oriented to Atlanta. But mentor A. J. Muste proposed making him southern secretary for the Fellowship of Reconciliation (FOR), the long-standing international Christian pacifist organization. Muste's FOR colleague Glenn Smiley suggested Lawson root himself in Nashville. While enrolled at Vanderbilt Divinity School, he represented FOR by venturing into hotspots like Birmingham and Little Rock during racial flareups to counsel Black activists. Indeed, the work served as fieldwork credit toward his degree.[3]

This aspect of Lawson's life portrays a wider if usually misunderstood aspect of civil rights history. His FOR work, typifying wider efforts to embed nonviolent direct action more deeply in Black activism, was hardly commonplace. The dramatic power and signature profile of nonviolent direct action associated with Martin Luther King Jr. has developed into a prevailing assumption of its widespread acceptance and deployment. But this was never the case, even in the 1950s and 1960s. Instead, the process of translating nonviolence to American racial contexts happened in uncertain fits and starts; "messy," "unsteady," and "experimental," as scholar Anthony C. Siracusa underlines. Black activists tried to work out nonviolence in theory, in practice, and as applicable to American society. Various groups systematically mulled how to actualize nonviolent direct action in thought and deed. They sought out Gandhian examples and Christian teachings, mixed them with other political traditions and mobilizations, and sought alliances with other pacifist and civil rights groups. Workshops remained a key element to that process, helping folks learn about nonviolence in theory and practice while customizing it to their beliefs, faith traditions, and ways of thinking. Lawson's version of that workshop process would enshrine Nashville's place in civil rights history.[4]

Nashville, when Lawson arrived in September 1958, had a particular racial climate that requires careful contextualization. It is not wrong to identify some small, discrete sites for racial goodwill and interaction within the city, mostly within educational, religious, and political sectors. Many attributed this to Nashville being home to a range of publishing and administrative headquarters for the Methodist and Southern Baptist churches, as well as the supposedly leavening effects of the many universities and colleges in town, which sometimes attracted people relatively more racially enlightened.[5]

Black institutions stood at the center of these spaces for integrationist possibility. The famed Race Relations Institute at Fisk University hosted annual interracial institutes and generated copious amounts of research. The meetings and data were intended to equip racial progressives with usable data about Jim Crow's effects and potential weak spots for attack. Faculty and staff at these schools were also active in the local NAACP chapter, which had a gifted attorney, Z. Alexander Looby. He set the pace in demanding racial change in the city throughout the 1940s and 1950s with continual lawsuits plus political work as a city councilman. His law partner Avon Williams had his own substantial career in law, civil rights, and politics in that generation and thereafter.[6]

Some white people played an auxiliary role, again usually in religious contexts. Will D. Campbell, representative for the National Council of Churches in Nashville, was an unusually progressive white minister who worked behind the scenes as a staunch resource for local civil rights activism. Campbell's secretary Dorothy Wood ended up marrying James Lawson. The United Church Women, Fellowship of Southern Churchmen, and the Tennessee Conference on Human Relations were similar groups active locally that tried to foster support for racial progress in step with local civil rights leaders. Kelly Miller Smith, the foremost figure among those Black ministers doing activist work in Nashville, pastored at First Baptist (Capitol Hill) Church and was a key facilitator of James Lawson's work.[7]

But, as always with Nashville, these realities must be heavily contextualized. Focusing on the conditions favoring racial possibility in the city must not overshadow how limited and proscribed those were. As Nashville reporter David Halberstam later put it, "There was more talk about change than change." The city's modest racial progress before 1960 underscored a strong and enduring white commitment to segregation across the city—including in those supposedly moderating dimensions of city life. Nashville's self-praise for being supposedly racially moderate was usually rhetorical posturing obscuring how quietly segregation was perpetuated, often through violence or the threat of violence. True progressive work was far more scant. Scattered examples of interracial worship, while positive, only affirmed themselves as the exception against firmer racial division persisting across the city's churches. The inroads made by Black voters mostly derived from concessions granted by the political machines that ruled the city. And the white economic elite from the banking, insurance, and manufacturing sectors that controlled the city smugly granted racial concessions only insofar as such allowances reinforced broader segregated patterns. Content in their splendored mansions in the rich enclave of Belle Meade, three miles of former plantation, Nashville's ruling class professed a mindset self-assured in its racial superiority—and equally the cultural, political, economic, and legal mechanisms in place to sustain that superiority. The city knew it did not need the rageful defiance of the Deep South to sustain white supremacy.[8]

Vanderbilt University encapsulated the city's spectrum of racial attitudes perfectly. As divided terrain, pockets of racial liberalism and avowed segregationist sentiment vied for influence against a more general backdrop of self-satisfied whiteness. During the twentieth century, clusters of white religious progressives calling for racial justice throughout the South had direct or indirect connections tracing back to Nashville and Vanderbilt, particularly the latter's Divinity School. These people had varying degrees of commitment. Some worked for more humane race relations within a separate-but-equal framework; others dreamed and worked for a more decisive break from the past. Such leaders included Willis D. Weatherford, working across fourteen states for the Young Men's Christian Association from 1902; Will W. Alexander, who spent twelve years in Nashville and directed the Southern-wide Commission on Interracial

Cooperation; Howard "Buck" Kester, Christian socialist and Vanderbilt graduate active in the Fellowship of Southern Churchmen; and Don West, who helped found the famed Highlander Folk School as a labor and civil rights workshop center in the Tennessee hills. Many of them were trained by Alva Taylor, an influential professor and proponent of the Social Gospel who worked at Vanderbilt Divinity School. Whatever limitations these people had in battling Jim Crow's cruel racial climate, they at least tried to represent the possibility of change.[9]

Yet Vanderbilt also hosted a small but influential conservative element during those same years. A group called The Fugitives, a version of a Southern literary salon, published a magazine in the early 1920s. Members also played key roles in the Southern Agrarian movement by contributing to the famed text *I'll Take My Stand*. This book of essays decried the scorn heaped on the South from outsiders, defending the region as an exemplar of traditional values threatened by the deadening and averaging effects of modernity and urbanity. In echoing many themes voiced in American literature both earlier and later, this volume stands as a notable addition to American letters, Yet the essays were also extremely reactionary and based on a thoroughly imaginary portrayal of Southern society and culture. And while some Agrarians later disavowed or ameliorated their beliefs—Pulitzer Prize–winning novelist Robert Penn Warren chief among them—the group nonetheless personified much of the tenor of campus intellectual life in the 1930s.[10]

The most racially recalcitrant of the Agrarians, a poet named Donald Davidson, taught in Vanderbilt's English Department. In the mid- to late 1950s, he chaired Tennessee's highest-profile segregationist group, the Tennessee Federation for Constitutional Government (TFCG). This group was at the forefront of segregationist energy across the state but especially in Nashville. Officers included a professor of romance languages from Vanderbilt, as well as the university's assistant business manager and a number of local attorneys. The organization maintained an elevated, respectable tone about states' rights and segregation, assiduously distancing itself from rabid promotors of violence. Yet the TFCG also quietly assisted those same proponents of violence with financial and legal support behind the scenes. And some TFCG members were prominent in hate groups that remain active today.[11]

With disparate viewpoints about segregation present on campus, Vanderbilt, like most Southern universities, was a place where racial inequality was both defended and questioned. But somehow only racial progressives were actively curbed by layers of control and repression. At Vanderbilt, at various times, Alva Taylor, Buck Kester, and Herman Nixon (an Agrarian who like Warren later adjusted his racial views), had been run off campus or at least were monitored by university officials. Indeed, purges of faculty members and students at other Nashville universities happened well into the 1960s. The same was not true for people like Donald Davidson, whose segregationist work was deemed insufficient for disciplinary action because he publicly eschewed racial violence. This sort of permissive double standard showcased the university's quiet comfort with segregation. And that mindset governing the university multiplied across the city, as Vanderbilt connections tied together the alumni who dominated the local business and political scenes, dictated the city's agendas, and reinforced white solidarity. The insular world of white supremacy thus replicated itself across campus and city.[12]

In the 1950s, challenges to that mentality heightened. Black activism, confronting discrimination directly on multiple fronts, saw their efforts gain some purchase. In higher education, both the federal government and national philanthropic organizations increasingly required documented signs of racial integration as a precondition for funding. With the need to modernize Southern universities, tapping these funds to overcome decades of relative underinvestment was imperative. For Vanderbilt in particular, the university's expansive growth after World War II meant tuition and endowment income remained insufficient to underwrite any ascent. Thus the university's reliance on grant money was paramount even with the strings of racial change attached.[13]

Various constituencies within Vanderbilt interpreted this dilemma differently. Many alumni harshly and vocally insisted that their university stay white-only. As Paul Conkin notes, the outcry was rarely based on moral or racial grounds. Instead, it was always voiced as an issue "of betrayal, of capitulation, of treason"—as a perceived violation of sacred white space. The Board of Trust understood the issue with less hysteria but nonetheless remained reflexively inclined against change. In 1960, the white Vanderbilt alumni who populated the Executive Committee of the board were, in their respective fields, prominent figures in the city and beyond. William Waller was a local attorney and keen historian. Jesse E. Wills, a member of The Fugitives poetry circle from the 1920s, mixed roles as a successful insurance executive and a supporter of local literary clubs and Vanderbilt's library. Influential banker and Chamber of Commerce member Sam Fleming was the great-grandson of a former Tennessee governor. John Sloan, a prominent businessman, owned one of the stores targeted by the lunch counter sit-ins in 1960.[14]

But two trustees were particularly germane to understanding civil rights history in the city. Both figured prominently in the Lawson Affair. James Stahlman, the archconservative editor of the *Nashville Banner*, had an avowed commitment to reactionary politics and racial segregation, often shrilly if colorfully articulated in his *Banner* newspaper editorials. An early diatribe on James Lawson, for example, castigated against "flannel-mouth agitators, white or colored"; a later one called Lawson's Christian witness "so much hogwash" that used Vanderbilt "to cloak his racial deviltry in clerical garb." The ability to steer public opinion, plus his deep involvement in Nashville's business and political circles, made some understand him as the most powerful man in the city.[15]

Attorney Cecil Sims, by contrast, wielded influence as a political and legal adviser, not just for Vanderbilt, nor only in Nashville, but across the South. Many of Nashville's biggest companies retained him as counsel. He was a major player in modernizing Vanderbilt Law School. He advised the Davidson County Board of Education and helped steer the metropolitan consolidation of the City of Nashville and Davidson County. He also advised the Southern Governors Conference about how to suppress the effects of court-ordered school desegregation. As with the rest of the trustees, Sims and Stahlman considered Vanderbilt to be, as scholar Melissa Kean put it, "extensions of their private domains, places for their children and their friends' children to make important social and business contacts under the paternal gaze of trusted guardians of the status quo."[16]

One non-Nashvillian, Harold S. Vanderbilt, presided over the Board of Trust. He was the great-grandson of the famous tycoon whose bestowal of funding started the university that bore his name. Mostly preoccupied with his stake in the family railroad empire and his nautical interests, Harold Vanderbilt had been wooed by Chancellor Harvie Branscomb and increasingly strengthened his relationship with the university. His support showed not only in time invested but also money; by 1955, his largesse and Ford Foundation grants constituted the two major income streams for the university.[17]

The man tasked with juggling these people and issues, Alabama-born Harvie Branscomb, was a lauded New Testament scholar and former head of the Duke University Divinity School. His scholarship, scrupulously neutral, betrayed no discernible evidence of religious belief. Early in his career, he had been fired from Southern Methodist University for defending an outspoken liberal colleague, although he had done so already holding his job offer from Duke. Like other leaders of elite Southern universities, the path that Branscomb faced in desegregating his university was challenging. Understanding both his disposition and the plight he faced is instructive.

Branscomb was committed to desegregating Vanderbilt and was moving, albeit gingerly, to do so. But—crucially—it had to be on his terms only. Managing a Board of Trust "deeply suspicious about innovation," plus recruiting an increasingly worldly and renowned faculty not inclined to work at a racially backward university, plus reassuring funding bodies about racial progress while negotiating a conservative student body with a reputation of being mostly "snobbish rich kids"—all required delicate care. Negotiating that balance was an evolving and ongoing calibration against competing demands. Melissa Kean argued that the chancellor believed in "moderation with content"—that is, he "staked out the middle ground in an effort to move all sides toward real, workable change." He had reached out to Nashville's Black community, albeit behind the scenes, and had carefully steered his Board of Trust toward a "controlled, limited loosening of racial restrictions" that led to "a series of minor but meaningful adjustments"—particularly, as we will see, aided by Vanderbilt's Divinity School.[18]

But temperamentally, Branscomb's capacity for fostering true integration was limited. He once told a story about entering a diner in New York City and seeing a Black patron eating there—he understood logically that his reaction came from an outdated racial upbringing but also admitted to instinctive feelings of nausea at the sight. His willingness to integrate had pronounced limits; it was confined to "the exceptional Negro," as Branscomb was "genuinely uncomfortable around lower class blacks" and highly disapproved of racial mixing. He especially "feared anyone with an idealistic agenda" where principles took precedence over pragmatism. Moreover, through the 1940s and 1950s, "racially pregnant" incidents stacked up. Branscomb's typical response to these dilemmas used carefully screened and exceptional candidates to facilitate bespoke and isolated examples of desegregation. He tailored this strategy to meet each moment without excessively changing conditions. Ushering in desegregation this way helped him reassure others accordingly. He could convince progressives and funders that progress was occurring; he could likewise persuade segregationists that actually little had changed. Such small infusions of token instances remained a common tactic widely deployed across the South. Despite instances of angry and violent white southern resistance grabbing headlines, tokenism was frequently more effective for preserving segregation.[19]

Vanderbilt's Divinity School helped Branscomb finesse these competing tensions by being a welcoming if contained space for Black students. A legacy of sorts remained from those past progressives at the Divinity School: there remained the commonly voiced notion that the school served as the moral voice for the university on racial matters. Whether that voice was listened to was a different question. Still, Joy Williamson-Lott, noted scholar of race in higher education, highlights in a different context how even limited dissent against the racial status quo mattered: "These battles represented cracks in the edifice of the Solid South." The Lawson case widened these cracks at Vanderbilt into chasms.[20]

In June 1952, Branscomb had dean of the Divinity School John Benton survey other theological schools about how they were desegregating student bodies. The results indicated that seminaries led the way, more so than schools of religion at Southern universities, but also revealed the wider pattern of limited acceptance even when Black students did matriculate. Sometimes enrollment was confined to denominational members, sometimes full privileges were permitted within the department but not the entire university. Other times Black students had specifically curtailed social privileges on campus. These precedents elsewhere gave Branscomb models to help plot his moves. Autumn 1952 witnessed a Divinity School faculty meeting rife with anxiety. Professors were threatening to resign if the school did not admit Black students. They drew inspiration from a similar tension-riddled gambit elsewhere in Tennessee, at Sewanee University's School of Theology. There, eight professors resigned on October 6, 1952, after the school rejected proposals to desegregate as "inadvisable." At the Divinity meeting, Branscomb and the Board of Trust announced formal approval for the Divinity School to admit Black students. Several months later, two Black students from nearby Scarritt College for Christian Workers enrolled at Vanderbilt due to an existing course-sharing agreement between the two schools.[21]

Regardless of the decisions managing desegregation from Kirkland Hall (the building housing the chancellor's office), the Divinity School operated from a strong position. It was thriving according to multiple criteria: student numbers were up, productive faculty members were visible leaders in their field, outward-facing links with religious institutions were being built. Some estimates categorized the school as one of the top five in the country. But these indicators of esteem were built on the trade-offs between successful grants income and desegregation that Branscomb carefully and profitably steered. In 1955, the school obtained a then-record grant of nearly three million dollars, including one million for new facilities. It was given only because Branscomb portrayed the Divinity School as a new beacon for progress in the South; the grant carried with it an implied requirement to enroll more Black students. This was one remit for the new dean of the Divinity School, J. Robert Nelson, who started in 1957. Although his first academic job, he came widely praised for his administrative and ecumenical abilities, seemed highly regarded by Branscomb, and continued enhancing the Divinity School's reputation until he became embroiled in the Lawson Affair.[22]

That first decision permitting the Divinity School to enroll Black students, however, was not publicly announced. Only private conversations and encouragement led Joseph Johnson, then president of Lane College in Jackson, Tennessee, who already had a doctoral degree, to apply successfully for admission in 1953. He finished the undergraduate degree in a year, applied to and was accepted for the PhD, and graduated in 1958. That silence was designed by Branscomb. So was the Board of Trust's directive that Vanderbilt would only admit Black students if their chosen program of study was not available at other schools nearby.

At the time, even that policy skirted legality. The Tennessee Code forbade white and Black citizens from being educated in the same school, classifying it as a misdemeanor subject to a fifty-dollar fine and up to six months of prison. Whether that law could be enforced, given recent changes in court rulings on education and race, was questionable, although it was very much a talking point for segregationist Vanderbilt alumni. Indeed, scholar Melissa Kean wrote that Branscomb seemed dismissive of Tennessee's segregation statutes, which he believed would not stand up under legal scrutiny for long. Vanderbilt historian Paul Conkin argued that Branscomb's stance was predicated on the hope that a legal test case would overturn segregation, opening up further opportunity for him but in fidelity to orderly judicial processes, as Branscomb understood "order as the prerequisite of any secure justice." Regardless, admitted Black students still faced other realities. They could only take religion classes and faced dictates about dining facilities and dormitories. Because of such issues, Joseph Johnson, a married man living off campus, was ideal. "In fact," one chronicler wrote, "most of the University and virtually everyone in the city knew nothing about the event until long after Johnson had graduated." These restrictions lifted only gradually in future years. The norm, in the meantime, was for a Divinity School faculty member to eat lunch with Black students in the dining hall to avoid potential issues.[23]

This racial trailblazing, a decisive break from tradition, marked a move, however slight, toward progress. It is just to celebrate those Black individuals who succeeded despite enduring constrained and humiliating circumstances. And yet such developments read differently when examining the capacity of institutions to change. When fully contextualized, these moves should be equally understood as a quiet amending of tradition for the sake of preserving a different version of segregation. That point is best shown by two people: Board of Trust member Cecil Sims and James Lawson himself.

The nature and meaning of Vanderbilt's desegregation is personified by Cecil Sims. He had made a career of advising politicians across the South, even before the *Brown* decision, about how conforming to legal rulings in the narrowest possible way would minimize racial progress. He had demurred from supporting Vanderbilt's desegregation of its Law School before the 1954 *Brown* decision. He waited until early 1955 to sponsor the motion that did so, in a manner similar to the Divinity School, accepting Frederick Taylor Work and Edward Melvin Porter Sr. starting in autumn 1956. This occurred despite howls of anger from Law School alumni. Sims orchestrated a similar process for Nashville's public schools, restricting integration to modest numbers while calculating new ways to stay functionally segregated while legally valid.[24]

Within the university, though, this maneuvering seemed invisible. Rooted in the supportive environment of the Divinity School, James Lawson's experience at Vanderbilt was by his own account pleasant:

> I found the Divinity School to be a very fine place; I knew the reputations of any number of the faculty people. I knew a number of them from Methodist student affairs and conferences and camps across the years in the Midwest and in the South. I had friends in the Board of Evangelism and in the Board of Education, both headquartered in Nashville, because I had served with them in different settings in the Methodist Church. So I felt myself very much at home in Nashville.

But comfort in his immediate circles could not mesh with Vanderbilt's continued commitment to segregation except for token exceptions. For

Lawson would not abide by the inhibited ways that Black people were supposed to remain on the margins across campus. They were not supposed to eat at university dining facilities nor attend Nashville Symphony events with their discounted student ticket prices, both of which Lawson did freely, and "these acts are known to have disturbed the university administration." A similar watchfulness had attended Lawson's decision to join the intramural football team. No outcry occurred, but precisely those situations made Branscomb fearful of a racial incident. Dean Nelson had notified Lawson about the chancellor's nervousness, albeit without pressure to change course.[25]

Lawson's academic studies at Vanderbilt were but one component of his continuing journey exploring how nonviolence could reshape Southern society. Not long after settling in Nashville, he began a series of workshops in his capacity with the Nashville Christian Leadership Conference (NCLC—the local affiliate to Martin Luther King's Southern Christian Leadership Conference, SCLC). He did so as local civil rights leaders mulled next steps after seeing both signs of progress and enhanced segregationist resolve in the city. Reverend C. T. Vivian, soon to be a staunch disciple of Lawson's nonviolent teachings, recalled that he once refused to move to the back of a segregated Nashville bus. This was shortly after the Supreme Court's 1956 *Browder v. Gayle* ruling outlawed the practice thanks to the Montgomery Bus Boycott. In his later telling,

> After a heated argument, the driver ordered everyone off the bus, except me. He then drove me to the police station. Believe it or not, the police did not know what the city's official policy was. They called City Hall and were told that post-*Browder*, Nashville was changing its rules regarding the segregation of public transportation. Henceforth, Blacks would not be required to take a back seat to our White brothers and sisters.[26]

Vivian's memory is noteworthy for several reasons. It showed how racial custom prevailed despite changes in laws. It showed how the bus driver maintained the right to police whiteness with support from law enforcement. It showed the uncertainties over how to actually enforce segregation, as demonstrated by the police officers' confusion. And it showed how ultimate decisions remained firmly in the hands of Nashville mayor Ben West. All these elements were integral to the Lawson Affair.

Regardless of that victory, the scale of civil rights challenges remained immense. This was true both in Nashville and across the South. After the buoyant triumphs of the *Brown v. Board* decision and the Montgomery Bus Boycott, a new climate of "massive resistance" among white Southerners descended across the region. Local and state politicians fed the backlash, busily applying legal, political, and social pressures wherever they could to quell civil rights momentum. Efforts to dampen progress on school desegregation, harass Black organizations, and shore up white resistance wherever possible had a chilling effect on racial activism.

A quintessentially Nashville version of this took place with the stalled effort to desegregate local public schools. Cecil Sims's adroit reading of the *Brown* decision suppressed integrated numbers to only minuscule levels after autumn 1957. Nashville professed superficial pride about taking that step but in actuality tolerated it with only the most grudging acquiescence. The city found itself caught in a vise. Relentless legal pressure from Z. Alexander Looby and the NAACP met shrill countermeasures from white parents goaded by a local organization affiliated with Donald Davidson's TFCG. In the high-stakes histrionics that overtook the city, an itinerant racial demagogue named John Kasper drifted into town, attracted large crowds, and whipped them into frenzied protest. Simultaneously, two integration-related bombings that thundered through the city signaled a situation that could no longer be controlled by city hall. Kasper's popularity threatened to expose the fraudulence of white Nashville's self-satisfied myth of amicable race relations to the wider world. His example made those on campus and across the city even more anxious about the current political temperature and inclined to brake racial progress.[27]

Given this diverse white resistance, the NCLC—like much of the Black Freedom Struggle across the country at this time—wrestled with what initiatives to take next, experimenting with voter registration drives, lobbying for Black employment opportunities, and appealing to white religious figures to rethink their commitment to segregation. A range of potential targets and proposed tactics showcased the enormous challenges civil right activists faced, with no obvious pathway opening up. But Lawson offered weekly meetings to discuss nonviolence with other ministers. These conversations soon deepened and extended into something altogether different.[28]

The early coffee chats later formalized into teaching workshops that dynamically distilled all that Lawson had learned up to that point. They featured interactive tutorials on nonviolence from varied historical, theological, and moral angles. For Lawson, the Methodism he was raised on provided a nurturing sense of self and belief, a "religious and intellectual foundation which shaped and bound together family, theological, ecclesiastical, and pacifist influences." One cannot ignore this profound influence on him personally. But scholars also underline how broadly he applied that template. Lawson took an all-encompassing view of Christianity. He sought to be a living embodiment of "humane values" rather than be preoccupied with religious structures or parsing theological issues. His reading of the Gospels and the redemptive example of Christ's selfless love, in his hands, chimed powerfully with a range of examples from Eastern and Western religions and philosophies. Each in different ways showed how faith traditions and commitments to higher values could transform political realities. He drew from diverse examples for workshop participants coming from different religious backgrounds and indeed those with profound skepticism about nonviolence.[29]

Lawson understood this instinctive attitude. He allowed these skeptics the space to think through the repercussions of nonviolence, to consider a new way, as his mother had instructed. He had a lifetime of his own reading, reflection, and experiences to lend to discussions. But others needed their own process. Several of the famed civil rights leaders who emerged from these workshops, including Diane Nash and James Bevel, were outwardly dismissive of nonviolence early on. Only over time, and with Lawson's tutelage, did their sentiments change. Although historians usually analyze these workshops in terms of their eventual success, the trajectory was much more fluid, organic, and open-ended—Lawson himself called the process an experiment.[30]

Rather than focusing on the end results of nonviolent protest, Lawson's workshops took a different emphasis. The crucial import of nonviolence came primarily from its innermost commitment. As he later discussed with an interviewer, adhering to nonviolence meant

> to help people see that they were of infinite worth and dignity. That their very life in fact was a center of the life of the universe, that the full power of what life is all about is located in every single human being. And no matter how tortuous that person's life is, they still have certain power if they're willing to exercise it and cultivate it and use it. And it may be risky, but it can be done.

In that sense, his experiment with nonviolence, no matter how much historical memory passes over the point, was intended primarily to stir Black belief, providing a template for actualizing faith into new forms of direct action. Only after this mobilization occurred did the growing opportunity to prick white consciences by asserting Black rights become a further avenue for pursuit.[31] Crucially for Lawson, however, the template for self could also apply to all of society's salvation. From that essential starting point of individual self-worth, he saw a natural continuation: where nonviolent direct action merged individual belief into a collective power to challenge injustice. A sense of self-worth, Lawson argued, must necessarily shape every interaction of one's life. With that belief, how could anyone continually defer and accept any limitations, large or small, that segregation imposed upon them in any given moment? As he put it, "each of us had a responsibility, in whatever way necessary, to begin to get liberated, begin to see that we had to organize to do it. The system cannot exist without our consent to it." The visible embodiment of equality and self-belief through nonviolent action radiated power, not weakness; a collective joining of that spirit could break barriers.[32]

In 1959, the workshops took on extra impetus after small numbers of university students from nearby Fisk and Tennessee State Universities joined. While still introducing the philosophical and theological bases for nonviolence, Lawson utilized a further technique to prepare his tutees by directing role-playing exercises. Some, pretending to be persecutors, shouted at and slapped the others, testing their composure for staying nonviolent under duress. By shaping their resilience, Lawson's students were better prepared for the violence that likely awaited. As Lawson conceived of it, nonviolent activism created a visual spectacle of resolve. But that in turn invited racial abuse directly, because violence, or the threat of violence, lurked constantly behind all interactions in a racially segregated society. Breaking norms nonviolently forced those violent realities to the surface, roiling tensions in hope of some sort of resolution.[33]

As the workshops continued, conversation often revolved around precisely that issue: how segregation's imposition created everyday forms of violence between Black and white sectors and within the Black community. Testimony from a Black housewife in one of Lawson's workshops triggered a shift from abstract knowledge to practical planning. As Lawson recalled her point, she said,

> You men don't really know what life is like in segregation. We are the ones who shop. When we go into downtown Nashville, there is no place that we can stop with dignity and rest our feet. There are no restrooms that are not marked either "Colored" period or "Colored Ladies." There's

> no place that one could sit down and have a cup of coffee. So as we do your shopping for you, you're often times in your own offices and the like, but we're the ones who bear the brunt of the racism of the segregation in Nashville.[34]

Thus everyday voices from the community reframed the crucial next steps. By asserting one facet of segregated injustice mostly invisible to the ministers and students, and finding widespread agreement, this woman awakened the NCLC to a tangible target. This was the first stepping stone in a plan to nonviolently desegregate all of downtown Nashville in the coming years. Beginning in May 1959, the students researched the companies owning the stores and held preliminary meetings with the merchants. Some were openly hostile; others were open to change but fretted about the rest of the city isolating and ostracizing them. A test-run requesting service at one lunch counter established that stores remained committed to policies of exclusion. A holiday lull and other commitments stalled developments. And then, news of the Greensboro, North Carolina, sit-ins reached them, and change seemed to beckon. Calls were made. Networks were activated. And the moment was ready to be seized.[35]

Despite the NCLC's preparations, and despite the fact that sit-ins had already taken place in Greensboro and in other Southern towns, Nashville's shock when the students moved was immense. On February 13, 1960, 124 students received a final set of instructions from Lawson, fanned out to different lunch counters in downtown, and—calmly, courteously, resolutely—placed their bodies in forbidden spaces. For them, it was like a baptism: they had crossed a segregated line and felt reborn because of it. The next two outings grew in size and intensity. Thursday, February 18, saw more than 200 students join in; Thursday the 20th had at least 350 participants. The business owners, befuddled, prevaricated by closing stores, removing counter stools, or stacking a literal wall on top of the lunch counters to demarcate the color line anew. As student protest fervor grew, so did the bristling rage of white onlookers who lurked along the margins of the demonstrations. Both sentiments percolated throughout the following week in expectation of what later became known as "Big Saturday."

The violence that erupted downtown on that day, February 27, dominated the headlines. But far more revealing interactions had already taken place. The store merchants, irate about being besieged for representing an entire society's racial mores, lobbied Mayor Ben West to fix the problem.

FIGURE 1.1. Now from a bygone era, the lunch counters were a potent symbol of segregation's hypocritical injustices given that Black people could buy items in the attached store, or take food away, but were not permitted by social custom to be seated to dine. *Nashville Banner* Archives, Special Collections Division, Nashville Public Library

James Stahlman was also livid about the demonstrations given his reactionary political leanings, commitment to segregation, and his ties to Nashville's business community. This pressure put West in grave political danger. His rise was based on an improbable fusion of support from Stahlman and the *Banner* but also Black voters. The latter had been personally courted by West for a number of years. Black votes not only enhanced West's attempt to paint Nashville as a forward-thinking city but provided the margin of victory in West's last election. As a result of the political predicament triggered by the sit-ins, the mayor had gone mysteriously missing ("heroically unavailable," as one reporter put it) to representatives from the Movement or from independent citizens' groups trying to reach him.[36]

FIGURE 1.2. The story of nonviolence in Nashville is not complete without understanding the ways individual and collective violence tested the protestors and reinforced segregation, both during protests and in daily life. *Nashville Banner* Archives, Special Collections Division, Nashville Public Library

The students readied themselves. A network of co-conspirators passed on the decision made from on high: that police would excuse themselves deliberately on Big Saturday, permitting white bystanders an unencumbered chance to attack the protestors. The students, meeting with chief of police Douglas Hosse, let him know that they would demonstrate that day, even though he promised to arrest them if they did. Indeed, in one retelling from Lawson, "he said that he had been instructed by the mayor to find what laws could be used" to do so. "And we made it clear to the chief of police then," Lawson later remembered, "that arresting us would not stop the movement and he needed to know that. But that was up to him and he was doing it illegally anyway." The potential crackdown highlighted a distinct change from West's quiet permissiveness about desegregated buses that C. T. Vivian had witnessed. The political costs of supporting a form of integration that touched white Nashvillians more directly had changed West's calculus. The students now faced extralegal violence as well as violence sanctioned by the state. With the stakes raised, they doubled down.[37]

As the sit-ins proceeded on Big Saturday, the events foretold came true. At each demonstration, tensions mounted as increasingly frustrated

FIGURE 1.3. "It reads the same on both sides." This cartoon embodies the classic moderate formulation that equated segregationist and civil rights unrest as equally taboo, even as events disproved that notion. Jack Knox, 1960. Image 222, box 6, folder 222, Jack Knox Papers, 1932–1978, Tennessee Historical Society Collection, Tennessee State Library and Archives, Nashville.

white observers escalated their anger. When the police in each store disappeared, forcefulness grew. Students sat impassively, remembering their training, unmoved as coffee and condiments poured over them. The confrontations boiled over into melees; fists replaced food; kicks and punches struck with building force. Throughout, students maintained nonviolent discipline. Only after the white bystanders started openly flailing at the protestors did police rush back into the stores—and arrested the seated students under attack. And yet, after those arrested were whisked off to jail, they were immediately replaced by a new round of demonstrators who briskly took up the newly vacated seats. The disciplined rotation stunned those who watched. Bewildered, then angered, the crowd resumed their harassment and spiraled into sporadic assaults again. At no point did the demonstrators fight back. In trying to test student resolve, Nashville's facade of white politeness lay in tatters among the scattered debris from the lunch counters.[38]

After 5 P.M., the police decided to restore their version of law and order. The entire downtown remained on edge. The arrested students filled Nashville's prison, mocking their punishment with songs and cheers. They knew the usual stigma of being jailed would not apply to their noble act. The following Monday saw a transparently ridiculous court session. One witness remembered how the judge would "deliberately swivel his chair and look at the wall behind him to demonstrate his disregard" for the defending attorneys. Two thousand Black Nashvillians waited outside the courthouse in solidarity with the students. Meanwhile, Mayor Ben West, who was notably out of town on Big Saturday, agreed to attend a meeting with Black ministers. These clergymen were incensed at the treatment of the students, ready to convey their displeasure, and eager to remind the mayor about exactly who had underwritten his recent electoral success. At that meeting, the case against James Lawson began being constructed.[39]

Big Saturday was big indeed: Lawson's students had passed their sternest test yet and taken their small step into history. For white Nashville, however, faced with this confounding method of mass protest, the disarray downtown prompted a fallback to time-honored stratagems of racial control. As reporters noted at the time, and as the Movement understood, even supposedly moderate Nashville condoned a reversion to the usual playbook of Southern repression when necessary: a police crackdown on baseless grounds, jail time to demoralize the activists and, finally, the targeting of a ringleader.[40]

2
Reckonings

FROM THE OUTSET, CONVERSATIONS about Lawson's role in the sit-ins were founded on mistruths. The manufactured racial turmoil in downtown Nashville on Big Saturday, aided and abetted by white Nashvillians in power, had a sequel in the pivotal meeting between Ben West and the Black ministers. Initially closed to the media, as Lawson preferred, West instead called for reporters to remain—a decision crucial for forthcoming developments. No complete transcript from this meeting exists, which requires details to be pieced together from newspaper coverage, fragmentary accounts, and oral histories. The latter two help establish how newspaper stories became deliberately weaponized against Lawson.[1]

In later interviews, Lawson recalled how the ministers grilled West: "'Why didn't the police protect our students? Why did they let this go on? Where were they? And why were you arresting them and you didn't arrest any white people who were in the mobs?' They really worked him over good." The mayor, twisting in the grip of an untenable political position, could only respond with platitudes. He reminded the audience about his opposition to John Kasper—a comparison in which, a reporter noted, the ministers "were no longer interested." West likened his stance against the racial demagogue to his current position on the sit-ins. Refusing to serve paying customers was not "fair," he allowed. But he could not permit anyone to "flout the law," regardless of "race, color or religion." West rationalized, "I do not think my Maker is going to judge you or me

FIGURE 2.1. "John Kasper learned the hard way." White Nashville frequently used John Kasper rhetorically as a reference point to rationalize their treatment of James Lawson. Jack Knox, 1960. Box 6, folder 238, Jack Knox Papers, 1932–1978, Tennessee Historical Society Collection, Tennessee State Library and Archives, Nashville.

by the color of our skin when we get up there. We are all alike. The only thing that makes us different is how we act." Whether West was repeating the banalities of many Southern moderates or using the ministers' own language of fairness and equality before God to defend his peculiar comparison with Kasper is hard to know. Regardless, he said little about those whites who actually broke the law during Big Saturday; he argued instead that sit-ins were legal until the lunch counter was closed, but any refusal to leave after that was illegal.[2]

It is necessary to pause on West's statement. The rhetorical ploy drawing an equivalency between anyone who disturbed the social peace, regardless of intent, was common in the Jim Crow South. After all, disavowing both segregationist violence and Black protest implicitly cherishes tranquility over change and thus preserves the existing order. But here, the comparison likened a racist fearmonger, actively calling for lynchings and riots to protect segregation, to avowedly nonviolent demonstrators who accepted beatings and jail in asking for societal change. And beyond that, the legal logic behind West's statement, professed with such certainty, was actually very much in doubt. The students were not trespassing, because the stores regularly welcomed them to shop or take food away. Only seating oneself, if one were Black, to eat at the counter was frowned upon, if technically not illegal. Nor were the students disturbing the peace or disorderly in conduct, given the fact, well-documented at the time, that only white onlookers resorted to violence. The charge of conspiring to disrupt commerce similarly made little sense, since the protestors wanted to contribute more business to the stores, not take it away.

Scholar Christopher W. Schmidt highlights how the timing of the 1960 sit-ins asked particularly telling legal questions. The use of the protest tactic at this specific historical moment struck precisely at the heart of a major constitutional ambiguity. In the North, discrimination in public accommodations routinely occurred in direct and ignored contradiction to laws explicitly forbidding such acts. Yet the South's array of Jim Crow legal restrictions had the opposite relationship to daily occurrences. Those laws explicitly requiring segregation in Dixie were either quietly being discarded or simply not enforced. As Schmidt put it, "Most of the privately owned lunch counters the students targeted were not compelled to discriminate by law. But they were also not required *not* to discriminate by law." Schmidt highlights that, as a result, "the key question then—the question to which there simply was no clear answer—was whether a private citizen who operated an eating facility, subject to no legal requirement to segregate, could make racially discriminatory choices of whom to serve."[3]

Resolving this matter meant addressing the tension between two major constitutional doctrines, both of which were in a state of evolution, as Schmidt also details. Legal rulings interpreting the state action clause, which delineates the Fourteenth Amendment's applicability to spheres of society, traditionally confined themselves to adjudicating matters of the state, not individuals. But recent Supreme Court decisions had steadily widened the clause's scope. Similarly, the equal protection clause, requiring consistent treatment under the law for all American citizens, was increasingly being applied to overrule segregation statutes. As such, the spectacle of the nonviolent sit-ins triggered a range of reactions. For some, it was moral soul-searching; others felt dismay or disgust or contempt. But among this public panic across wider white society, there was also confusion—especially legally so.[4]

Maybe West believed what he said. Perhaps he merely seized on a convenient answer to mollify conflicting constituencies and preserve his career. Certainly, many white people in 1960 believed without question that segregating lunch counters was constitutionally valid. It was an article of faith that one's business was an extension of the individual. But, in this situation, that accepted knowledge was debatable as a matter of principle and of law. Those stores that sold sundry items and served food at lunch counters existed in a legal gray area, a zone of contested constitutional interpretations differing about where public and private spheres overlapped. Given those overlaps, the extent to which the state was required to impose equality in those spaces remained contested. Even if a store owner was, legally speaking, permitted to segregate, being licensed by the state, serving a general public, and using police resources to enforce such discrimination made that stance a state matter. As Schmidt put it, "in modern society there is no unproblematic, neutral manner by which the line between the public and private spheres can be drawn." As such, "the public-private distinction on which the state action doctrine relies is not a fact. It is a decision. It is a legal construct. In practically any situation that might arise as a site of significant social contestation, state involvement of some sort can be located." Or, as Lawson later phrased it archly, "you can't have a public store one minute and a private store the next."[5]

For Nashville's lunch counters, the mishmash of laws imposed over decades to enforce racial segregation still had gaps. The city attorney maintained that no city ordinance required segregation. The local district attorney said that any segregation policy was entirely at the owner's discretion. One journalist pressing the issue found that the only law on the books was a segregation regulation mandated by the Tennessee hotel and restaurant division. The director of that division demurred about how such a regulation might be enforced but stressed that "it has the force of law."[6]

The disarray of these answers showed an essential contradiction that the sit-ins magnified directly. Here the Movement's legal understanding matched its moral clarity. Thus Lawson could not permit such half-baked rationalizations to dictate the discourse with the mayor. Since West condemned the sit-ins in terms of law-breaking, Lawson had to reject the very premise. His foremost point wished to stress the moral imperative of the sit-ins as an outright rejection of Jim Crow. But Lawson noted that, even as the mayor spoke in terms of trespassing, the students were actually arrested on charges of disorderly conduct. Lawson also was addressing how specific local laws in the South had recently been introduced to "circumvent the effect" of federal desegregation efforts. His specific rejoinder to West is lost to history. He later paraphrased it in an oral history: "the arrests occurred, not because the law was an effort to preserve the finest values of our society, but in this instance the law was a gimmick to intimidate, harass, and if possible, halt a legitimate movement of social concern and justice."[7]

The phrasing critiqued white supremacy, called out the transparent ways that white citizens used fictions of legal standing to maintain racial control, and disavowed the willful misreading of the sit-ins' messaging. Later Lawson explained that the narrow obsession with legal interpretations from white people helped ignore the morality at stake. Dialoguing about lawfulness was beside the point. Any charges of trespassing and disorderly conduct were "moot" because laws mandating or enforcing segregation were both unconstitutional and immoral, used "as weapons of intimidation to force people to comply with immoral practices." Civil disobedience was necessary to thwart these legal structures that reinforced racial custom. This, of course, was entirely faithful to Lawson's vision of nonviolence: a willingness to break unjust laws so as to dramatize that injustice, and to embrace paying the legal penalty for doing so. One broke unjust laws as the mark of ultimate respect for the law's ability to facilitate justice, even as nonviolent spectacles created potent visuals to make a moral point.[8]

But only some heard Lawson's response for what it was. Immediately, despite the cries of support for Lawson's stance, West alighted upon the "gimmick" phrasing as suggestive of something else. "I hope I didn't hear what this man said," West said, "because he is calling for a bloodbath in the streets of Nashville." This distortion of Lawson's wording prompted Lawson's colleagues to verbally and aggressively refute the mayor's interpretation immediately as it was voiced. But perhaps the ministers were not the intended audience.[9]

Media present at the meeting helped this distortion take on a life of its own. The key version, featuring prominently in Stahlman's subsequent *Banner* coverage, was furnished as damning evidence. This account

FIGURE 2.2. The extent to which the *Nashville Banner* was loathed by most of Black Nashville for its shrill defending of Jim Crow was only heightened by how editor James Stahlman relentlessly targeted James Lawson for his activism. *Nashville Banner* Archives, Special Collections Division, Nashville Public Library

suggested that Lawson "will continue to advise students to 'violate the law,'" and quoted him as saying that the law "is being used as a gimmick." (Printed above an editorial bellowing against Lawson was the Biblical thought for the day, Galatians 6:10: "As we have therefore opportunity, let us do good unto all men, especially unto them who are of the household of faith.") The *Banner*'s cross-town rival, the *Tennessean*, was moderate only in contrast to the *Banner*, with a stable of reporters who ranged widely in their racial views while being supervised by a conservative editor. Regardless of that spectrum, the *Tennessean* and Mayor West were political rivals, which also colored that newspaper's reporting. Certainly much of the *Tennessean*'s coverage seemed to treat Lawson in targeted ways, and editorially the paper disapproved of the sit-ins. But Lawson's specific quotation from the West meeting differed; the *Tennessean*'s coverage had Lawson saying instead that "the law has been a gimmick to manipulate the Negro and keep him in his place in the South." As such, "the students have made a definite decision to violate this legal gimmick." In this version, the emphasis clearly stressed that the students were challenging unjust laws, as opposed to the *Banner*'s rendition of Lawson's supposedly wide-ranging avowal.[10]

The account in the *Chattanooga Times*, a newspaper entirely removed from the internal media politics of Nashville, highlighted the contrast all the more. Skewing more toward the *Tennessean*, the *Times* quoted Lawson as saying, "the law has been used as a gimmick to keep the Negro in his place. The students have decided they cannot do other than violate the law and remain on the premises of these stores when the law is used to crush the rights of our people." Weeks later, one administrative adviser to Branscomb compared these newspaper accounts with notes from reporters present at the meeting. He allowed that the Chattanooga article "would have prevented the whole trouble over Lawson." But it was too late. The *Banner*'s coverage embedded a particular narrative about Lawson into public discourse to set up further action from the Vanderbilt Board of Trust, which, it will be remembered, had not only Stahlman on the Executive Committee but also John Sloan, the lunch-counter owner most resistant to desegregation.[11]

News of the melees downtown had quickly circulated to campus. The outrage from Nashville's power structure caused consternation among university officials. Some accounts claimed that Mayor West had leaned on Branscomb directly, although certainly Stahlman would have been a factor. J. Robert Nelson, dean of Vanderbilt Divinity School, was soon swept into the maelstrom. Despite suffering from influenza, Nelson remained active that weekend. On Sunday, he preached twice at First Presbyterian Church, asking parishioners to pray over the meaning of the sit-ins, and later attended a meeting of the Tennessee Council of Human Relations to work on a statement protesting white violence on Big Saturday. On Monday, he read the newspaper coverage of Lawson and talked to Branscomb on the phone as the chancellor gathered information. Nelson vouched for Lawson's character. Just before hanging up, Branscomb asked, "Oh, is he a Negro?" Nelson answered by reminding Branscomb about their previous conversations stemming from Lawson joining the intramural football team.[12]

The following day, Nelson got another call from Will D. Campbell, who had grasped that the news coverage was setting Lawson up as a convenient target. So Nelson hurried to campus and found Lawson, who understandably objected to the media's portrayal. He claimed that "the words he spoke at the ministers' meeting were woven into a later exchange with West" and that the issue of law was "not made clear in the meeting" since West had been talking about trespassing on store property. Nelson immediately suggested that Lawson write a statement. He later recalled that, in discussing this, Lawson offered to withdraw from Vanderbilt. This offer, put in writing, was later destroyed, although Nelson held out hope that he could arrange a different outcome. As Lawson began his draft, Nelson met with Branscomb and his chief advisers, having a conversation that was, in Nelson's view, "very desultory, sometimes pointless." Their singular focus was on lawlessness, despite being well aware that Vanderbilt itself was breaking the law by having integrated classes.[13]

The chancellor instead zeroed in on a university regulation decreeing that any student present at the scene of an unruly crowd was subject to punishment, regardless of the extent of their participation. This argument, central to later rationalizations, was faintly absurd both procedurally and morally. The regulation's origins stemmed from May 1958 after a bout of campus rowdiness where hundreds of male students, upset by Branscomb's efforts to curtail the Greek system, twice staged unsuccessful if persistent panty raids, scaling walls to get into female dormitories. The regulation's intent to guard against such undergraduate hijinks from the era was so transparent it was never formally applied to graduate student procedures. Another point quickly cast aside was that Lawson never actually physically participated in the sit-ins downtown; on Big Saturday he stayed at First Baptist to help coordinate the Movement's responses. Nonetheless, the outcome from Nelson's meeting with Branscomb was that the university required Lawson to clarify his position, specify whether he was "misquoted or only misrepresented" by the media, and proclaim that he would adhere to the so-called "anti-mob rule." The idea was to "urge Lawson to be a real reconciler in this difficult situation."[14]

Nelson worried about Lawson's response and indeed Branscomb was displeased upon reading it, as he found it "evasive." In this document, Lawson wrote of his "regret" about the "widespread misimpression that I advocate lawlessness or the incitement to riot." He reaffirmed his belief in a "system and practice of law which preserves both the safety and rights of all its members." He specified that the sit-ins' purpose meant to "invite the genuine concern" from the city about Nashville's lunch-counter segregation. Nelson understood Lawson's dilemma: the activist wanted to defend his lifelong devotion to nonviolence, highlight the ambiguous legal status of the lunch counters, and most of all not obscure how the sit-ins were emphasizing the immorality of segregation—all while trying "to clear his name" and stress that he was "not an anarchist" as he was being portrayed.[15]

After the chancellor brought up the panty raid rule again, which

Nelson thought little of, the dean nonetheless picked up on Branscomb's thinking and saw an opening. He volunteered to ask Lawson to acquiesce to the rule and refrain from the sit-ins until his June graduation. The dean figured this might be "the legal technicality" permitting Lawson to stay enrolled, which was apparently Nelson's paramount if misplaced priority. Nelson "hoped that out of respect for the university and Divinity School in particular [Lawson] would agree." With this, he asked Lawson to consider voluntarily withdrawing and to write a new statement "disavowing alleged lawlessness" plus "expressing appreciation for VU and efforts for integrating and expressing feelings for the Divinity school."[16]

As discussions continued, Lawson's dismay grew. "The issues as they were posed to me," he recalled, "changed very rapidly" as Nelson returned from successive meetings. Nevertheless, he would not desert the Movement. He had initially offered to withdraw, and went so far as to draft that paragraph declaring so, because he worried about adverse publicity for Vanderbilt after the West meeting. Occasionally his offer was brought up and then dropped. But now Lawson realized that withdrawing would only solidify the false media narrative about his intentions. It would permit Vanderbilt to ignore Lawson's own explanations for his actions and bypass formal protocols for student discipline. He found himself annoyed with Nelson's suggestion that promising to abide by the "panty raid rule" would be diplomatically useful. That insulted the Movement's motivations and, Lawson thought, facilitated his persecution for the mere fact that a "lawful and responsible Christian movement . . . had been falsely characterized in the press of Nashville."[17]

Given this impasse, the pair worked on another statement. It was, as Nelson knew, "very bad luck" that the Executive Committee had a previously scheduled meeting that afternoon. While the main agenda item concerned the launching of the university's first major mass fundraising drive, Lawson would unquestionably be a topic of conversation. For this new statement, Lawson dictated his response as if addressing friends in the Divinity School. In this more pointed draft, he criticized the media coverage and described his "intense embarrassment because, in the public's eye, I have been made what I am not." Instead, Lawson explained that "defiant violation of the law is a contradiction of my entire understanding of the loyalty to Christian nonviolence." He explained that "when the Christian considers the concept of civil disobedience as an aspect of nonviolence, it is only with the context of a law or a law enforcement agency which has in reality ceased to be the Law, and then the Christian does so only in fear and trembling before God." Indeed, "the sit-in has never intended to invite a riot or the breakdown of public order and, for my part, will never do so."[18]

The statement was team-edited with Vanderbilt official Robert A. McGaw, with Nelson often siding with Lawson on sections that McGaw questioned. Lawson kept adding extended passages elaborating on his theology, even as Nelson tried to keep the language concise to lessen the risk of being misunderstood. At this point, Lawson later recounted, "I was tired and frustrated and felt that I had been trying to defend myself against unknown accusers and false allegations. I had felt from the beginning that to try and defend oneself against such gross distortions was of little value anyhow." He wanted to return to the Movement instead. In his account, he said that Nelson "stated this was a good statement, it satisfied him, and he felt that we understood each other" and that "he was fully prepared to defend it." Nelson by contrast wrote that, as a "theological statement of motivation and purpose," the wording was "superb testimony," but worried that it would not placate the Executive Committee. He suspected that the trustees would not sanction the contradiction of Lawson renouncing "lawbreakers" while still declaring that civil disobedience, including lawbreaking, could be tied to higher justifications. The balance between articulating principles faithfully while speaking to a hostile audience could not be maintained, especially with Nelson trying to keep Lawson in school while Lawson remained determined to maintain his moral grounding. All intentions worked at cross purposes.[19]

The Executive Committee meeting to decide Lawson's fate occurred on Ash Wednesday, March 2. Nelson recalled later that, upon arriving for lunch, members were reading the *Banner* editorial "likening Lawson to Kasper and demanding his expulsion." As the meeting began, Nelson later wrote that he opened with a reminder for those in attendance about Ash Wednesday's theological significance: a "day of remembrance of that time when our Lord went towards his death for breaking the law" and "a time for general penitence." Other accounts remembered Nelson saying instead that he felt like Christ before Pontius Pilate, which came across as a "gratuitous insult." In presenting Lawson's case, Nelson specifically discussed the minister as a Divinity student to downplay the association with the sit-ins, although he explained Lawson's affiliation with the Fellowship of Reconciliation. He also professed his doubts about the university regulation's applicability and his personal view that Lawson's mission to eradicate segregation was just. As McGaw read Lawson's statement, the cry of "there it is!" came from a board member responding to Lawson's wording about civil disobedience. The ensuing conversation, in Nelson's estimation, coupled "vehement" statements about the "need for law and order" with expressions of "indignation" that anyone might deign to be the "judge of when a law is binding and when it is not, even when convinced that he knows the higher law of God." And Lawson's "fear and trembling" line was understood as an intention to continue practicing civil disobedience, which of course was very much the case.[20]

Members also discussed Lawson's imprisonment during the Korean War. Nelson had rather clumsily tried to get this information removed from Lawson's admissions file, thinking that it would be used unfairly against Lawson, but to no avail. The dean later noted that the *Banner* ran this news about Lawson's past in the next day's coverage. Many felt that Stahlman, a World War I veteran, was particularly furious over Lawson's choice to avoid military service. Moreover, some present at the meeting found out about Nelson's ill-advised if well-intentioned act and deemed it proof of nefarious motives. More importantly, they interpreted Lawson's criminal record as further evidence of a willingness to ignore the law.[21]

Nelson recorded Cecil Sims as articulating a very particular set of truths and assumptions: 1) that Lawson "forced the university into the position of either sponsoring him or having him withdraw"; 2) that Lawson, however "honest and intelligent," was a "zealot with intense purpose and strategy"; and that 3) it was a criminal offense to trespass on another's property and thus Lawson was liable for arrest, and yet Sims had it on "good authority that Lawson would not be arrested, lest he be thought even more a martyr." Number 2 was unquestionably accurate; Number 1 dubious at best. And Number 3 was completely misguided, as events soon showed—as misguided as Sim's assertation that his attempts to trace the origins of the typewriter ribbon used to make flyers for the sit-ins suggested that it may have come from the Divinity School.[22]

Branscomb's summary of the committee's collective position was that those acting on principles of civil disobedience (as opposed to endorsing them in the abstract) and who broke the law ("or conspired to do so") could not be supported by Vanderbilt and thus the university must "sever connections with Lawson." The question, then, was the appropriate course of resultant action. Potential penalties ranged from suspension to expulsion, although Branscomb was mindful that suspension presumed the possibility of reinstatement.[23]

When the committee turned to Nelson for advice, he understood that there was no way Lawson would be permitted to stay in school. He feared the costs of that act for the university's and Divinity School's reputations, as this was the "first time [the Executive Committee] ever made a decision on internal policy or student discipline." So he asked instead to defer the decision, noting instead that Lawson had mentioned the possibility of withdrawing. He offered to broker such an arrangement with Lawson with the understanding that refusal would lead to expulsion. The committee approved, with at least one person expressing sympathy for Nelson's task.[24]

Around six o'clock that evening, Nelson notified Lawson that the Executive Committee had decided on withdrawal or expulsion. He had a statement requesting the same, justifying it on the basis of Lawson's "strong commitment to a planned campaign of civil disobedience." He stressed the conservatism of the Executive Committee "and how futile it was to think that the radical notion of Christian nonviolent civil disobedience could be accepted by them as a legitimate conviction or policy." In asking Lawson to choose withdrawal, Nelson clarified that he was "not coercing" him but rather following up on Lawson's previous offer; he "offered to get on his knees" as "he saw no other alternative." He also conjectured that Lawson might cost the university tens of millions of dollars with the university's imminent funding drive, which no one had suggested. The dean's logic was that Lawson could spare the university and the Divinity School further negative headlines by preventing the university's "terrible action" while still working on behalf of racial justice. He also answered Lawson's question by advising that an expulsion on his scholastic record would doom any transfer to another school—a point that "he did not want to use as leverage" and was, as events later proved, completely wrong. Despite Nelson's best intentions and genuinely warm relationship with Lawson, he was still in effect asking Lawson to save the university from its own mistakes.[25]

Lawson refused to sign. He needed time to ponder. He reiterated that withdrawing meant that the biased press coverage, the lack of a hearing to defend himself, Vanderbilt's neglect of his own student rights, and his commitment to the Movement all remained substantial issues ignored by this ultimatum. After agreeing to provide an answer by 9 A.M. the next day, the two prayed together, "or rather I said the prayer," Nelson later wrote, "which was as real and agonizing as any I have ever uttered." For Lawson, the turn of events was devastating. His life of Christian witness was now being depicted as destructive to one of the very places that had nourished that growth. Hurt by the personal attacks and misrepresentation, painted as the scourge of a place that he loved, he was depressed, beaten down, and ready to wash his hands of the whole thing. He asked

Will Campbell to edit his withdrawal statement. But Campbell, who had been chased out of the University of Mississippi due to his own racial activism, would not have it. Lawson was the victim here and Vanderbilt was in the wrong, he insisted. Do not give them what they want: "make them kick you out so that they and the world will know."[26]

The next morning, awaiting Lawson's response while both Branscomb and Harold S. Vanderbilt pushed Nelson for an answer, the dean remembered how he "sobbed convulsively" and again "went to pray" in the school chapel. He heard the university clock "chime nine, and I knew it was too late." Not until 9:15 did Lawson reach Nelson, telling him that he was still working on his statement and claiming that the phone had been busy. Nelson's response was that the university at this point was "not much interested" in the statement and that Lawson "had let me down."[27]

Thus Vanderbilt University dismissed the Reverend James Lawson. After meeting for nearly four hours, and absent a formal reply from Lawson, the Executive Committee voted unanimously for expulsion. The statement released by Branscomb cited the university's "obligations incident to its charter from the State of Tennessee and its membership in a society organized under law" and specified that, rather than a question of academic freedom or the right to demonstrate, the issue instead was "whether or not the university can be identified with a continuing campaign of mass disobedience of law as a means of protest." The chancellor noted that the university would continue to admit qualified Black applicants and highlighted that Lawson's expulsion came not from "the expression of ideas," which he claimed the university would have protected, but rather "continued actions." In other words, as Nelson later noted, Vanderbilt dismissed Lawson not for "violating the 'panty raid' rule but refusing to agree to abide by it."[28]

On the next day, March 4, Lawson was arrested—according to his design, especially given that the press had advance notice that he would be detained—at First Baptist Capitol Hill Church. The warrant charged him with conspiring to violate state commerce laws. Initially the protestors had been arrested for inciting a riot, a decision later deemed legally iffy. So a deliberate effort to find a better law to use, and one that could also apply to Lawson, had ensued. The arresting cops refused to douse their cigars or remove their hats as they entered the sanctuary. As reporter David Halberstam wrote, "they handled Jim as harshly as they could, until finally Lawson's wife shouted 'Why do you have to be so rough! Why are you trying to hurt him! Why do you have to do it this way? He

FIGURE 2.3. Iconic photographs helped amplify James Lawson's nonviolent stance to a wider audience. He was later quoted as feeling "a vast sense of relief" with his arrest given his varied tribulations after the *Banner* attacked him editorially and Vanderbilt University failed to defend him. *Nashville Banner* Archives, Special Collections Division, Nashville Public Library

isn't resisting!'" A now iconic image captured Lawson being escorted to a police van in front of the noticeboard announcing the week's sermon: "Father, Forgive Them."[29]

After Lawson's arrest, the war of words multiplied. Newspaper coverage was deeply implicated in the shaping of developments and responses. Stahlman, having already laid the purported rationale for Lawson's expulsion with the *Banner*'s coverage of the West meeting, quickly chimed in with editorial approval: "With that decision, justice assuredly concurs." By disassociating the act from Vanderbilt's policy of admitting Black students, the editorial sought to strip the case of its racial implications and further pinned the expulsion on Lawson's "avowal of intent to continue 'a program of civil disobedience.'" By rejecting law and order, Stahlman wrote, Lawson had violated "the very framework of orderly government, and public security innate to it," and, as an institution of higher education, Vanderbilt's responsibility was "to cultivate standards that are the bedrock of citizenship." The institution could not "abet by sufferance or by silence eccentric interpretations" of those using "a wresting of either law or scripture to suit his own apotheosis." Additional coverage from the *Banner* included Lawson's statement in full but also highlighted Lawson's previous arrest for violating the Selective Service Act. While noting that the prison was used for conscientious objectors, it otherwise failed to detail Lawson's principled stand leading to that arrest. The *Banner* likewise opted to reprint supportive editorials from other newspapers suggesting that logical consistency required the disavowal of law-breaking by segregationists and integrationists alike. Branscomb later repeatedly used this same argument. Stahlman also sent his reporters digging for material from Lawson's past to aid a potential smear campaign. At the same time, a range of bogus rumors about Lawson began to circulate around Vanderbilt's campus, to say nothing about the daily phone calls threatening his life.[30]

Civil rights activists and their supporters pushed back. The NCLC scolded Branscomb for focusing on Lawson's statement to the mayor, who "put words into Lawson's mouth." The group noted that constitutionally the minister was quite correct: "no local ordinance or state statute . . . can legitimately be invoked against the sit-ins without violating the constitutional rights of private citizens." The NCLC pointed out that, given that the sit-ins rested on legitimate legal grounds, the police were enforcing invalid laws, especially since local and state laws conflicted with federal rulings. And the civil rights group further noted that, since Branscomb had violated state law in overseeing Vanderbilt's desegregation, the university was presumably as guilty as Lawson. Local Black newspapers echoed the charge. The *Nashville Globe* editorialized that "only Satan himself will be willing to stand up and cheer" for Vanderbilt, and the *Nashville News Star*, eager to highlight the racial implications of the expulsion, wrote that "when the mob, acting on this image, shouted 'Barabbas,' Branscomb and his board joined the chorus."[31]

There was wider support for Lawson. His professors pooled together money to pay Lawson's bail, although it was not a given that Lawson would accept it.[32] Eleven Divinity School members then issued a statement suggesting there was "no adequate justification" for the university's actions and days later announced the Lawson Faculty Defense Fund. Divinity School graduate students added their own statement of support, in contrast with the Vanderbilt Student Senate who publicly backed Branscomb. On March 9, the *Tennessean* ran a statement from 111 Vanderbilt professors that "deplore[d] the intolerance that is the fundamental cause" of the current crises. The statement pointed out that the legal status of the sit-ins, still pending before the courts, remained open to interpretation. They also asked for equal consideration about the legal and moral dimensions of the protests. The signees were "distressed" by Vanderbilt's actions, which supported "the denial of rights of Nashville Negroes." This was answered by a counter-petition with ninety-seven names supporting Branscomb, and these numbers included "majority support" from the engineering and medical schools plus the English department. Different constituencies were banding together either for or against Lawson's expulsion. The fluidity of Nashville's race relations under these moments of social stress divided people into warring camps.[33]

Everyone had an opinion on the crisis. The issue remained live in part because of how the media continued to actively shape public conversations. Certainly, the coming months demonstrated that leaks to both the *Banner* and *Tennessean* were frequently being used to steer public perceptions. The Divinity faculty noticed that they usually learned about developments on campus by reading the newspaper rather than via university communications. They also noted the virtually identical language used by Branscomb and the *Banner*. But mainstream national outlets picked up the Lawson story too. *Time* magazine described Branscomb as a Southern liberal, stressing his work to convince the board to desegregate in 1953, and called him "personally sympathetic to the sit-in strikers' goals." But, added the magazine, "'civil disobedience' is something else again. Branscomb firmly believes that whites and Negroes must equally obey the law—or face race riots." The newspaper quoted without comment Lawson's retort that the sit-ins directly targeted a statute that "in reality has ceased to be the law." By contrast, *The Washington Post* later commented sarcastically that "this is what comes of allowing Christian doctrine to be taught in such places. . . . Vanderbilt University's trustees seem to have decided that they are not going to tolerate any more of this sort of Christian morality in their Divinity School."[34]

More focused national outcries were aided by one Divinity School professor, Everett Tilson. Already more progressively inclined and spurred by a job offer elsewhere, Tilson felt like he had been blacklisted by Branscomb after hosting a 1957 conference on the church and race that had garnered national publicity. As such, Tilson pushed for sympathetic media coverage, extensively lobbying friends, journalists, and religious liberals to voice their disapproval of Vanderbilt publicly in letters to the editor and similar forums. In particular, he maintained continuous correspondence with editors at *The Christian Century*, whose editorials consistently voiced disapproval about the "cold disregard" for Lawson and argued that the sit-ins were inextricably linked to Lawson's role as a Methodist pastor. Noting that the "wisdom and justice of [the expulsion] is highly questionable," the periodical asked if "perhaps this is a fitting time to ask whether a university is the handmaid of the culture in which it finds itself or the champion of the ethos in which men may seek and find and live by the truth." Tilson thanked the editor directly: "nobody has covered the affair so perceptively or fully."[35]

The ongoing media storm only continued over the coming weeks. But these outcries ran parallel to quieter developments on campus, a second and nearly separate phase to the entire episode. Here, bubbling undercurrents of tension within the Divinity School were one part of the story. Another was the quiet disapproval from other professors on campus about the expulsion and what it meant. And a third was Branscomb's responses to both while still trying to manage the aftereffects from the expulsion. The convergence of these factors slowly and inexorably deepened the crisis even while spiraling away from the particulars of Lawson's situation.

Lawson's expulsion had stirred personal and professional apprehensions among members of the Divinity School faculty. In rushing between Lawson and Kirkland Hall, Nelson had belatedly shared only sparse updates with his colleagues, including his initial instinct that an expulsion was unlikely. The professors had previously remained slightly aloof from the sit-ins; a few were only dimly aware that Lawson was instrumental to the campaign. Occasionally the issue arose at lunchtime conversation and at least some had voiced some reservations about the tactic even though they favored integration. But now these professors were questioning those opinions in light of Lawson's punishment. Colleagues passed a note to Nelson before the fateful Executive Committee meeting, supporting him in this difficult position but warning that an expulsion might prompt their resignations. While Nelson had argued for the chance to consult with his colleagues about the order, he never shared the specific threat of resignations with Branscomb or the Executive Committee. Now anger was manifest. Some of the professors were conscious that Lawson's civil disobedience was "consistent with certain Christian ethical insights taught in the Divinity School." Plus they resented both the lack of consultation and the hard-line decision.[36]

After the Executive Committee's vote, Branscomb had to defend the decision to various constituencies. One tart-tongued academic asked the chancellor "if Gandhi could have studied at Vanderbilt." The Divinity School faculty "exploded with dismay" at the news, warning Branscomb that the university's reputation "would stink to high heaven around the world." Bizarrely, the chancellor never formally notified Lawson in writing; instead, he announced the decision impersonally to the minister while meeting with the entire Divinity School student body. Standing before them, he said, "Mr. Lawson, I do not know who you are, I have never met you, but I understand you are present. You are no longer a student in this university." Given that this proved that the chancellor had not consulted with Lawson directly, his subsequent explanations for the act were met with "sardonic laughter" from the students. Branscomb's response to one student, asking if Vanderbilt had broken Tennessee law by desegregating, was equally discrediting. This was not an abstract question, given that Highlander Folk School in East Tennessee, a space for labor and civil rights activist workshops, had recently been ordered to shut down based on that statute. Branscomb replied that the state ordinance had "ceased to be law" given the *Brown v. Board* ruling. After Branscomb left, Lawson took the floor and reiterated that the university's actions stemmed from a media caricature of him. He also made the case that his nonviolent teachings had actually kept Big Saturday's turbulence from being far worse.[37]

Increasingly peeved with the outcry against the expulsion, Branscomb's annoyance now turned to Nelson as much as Lawson. The dean's stumbled attempts to resolve the situation now gave way to a growing willingness to express his dissatisfaction. But that U-turn made Branscomb seethe, particularly as events tended to cast Nelson in a favorable light compared to Branscomb. The chancellor was furious that Nelson did not do more before the Executive Committee to make his case, and his mood only worsened as Nelson actively spoke out against the chancellor. "So he felt he was sandbagged by Nelson," one person recalled; "Harvie really was hurt and bothered by Nelson, this was the thing that people never quite realized." Both Nelson and a colleague criticized Branscomb strongly at a University Senate meeting in mid-March, questioning the lack of adherence to proper procedures and noting inconsistencies in the rationale for Lawson's expulsion. In particular, and perhaps in a bid for allies, they highlighted Lawson's case as one about academic freedom as much as civil disobedience. Besides, given that Lawson's expulsion stemmed from his "failure to give assurances about future behavior," they argued that Lawson's theory of moral action was a legitimate matter for discussion. The presentation led one of Branscomb's staff to quietly call the professors "insubordinate." It also prompted the chancellor's remark to a bystander musing about closing the Divinity School and returning the recent grant that had bankrolled its expansion. Nonetheless, he kept trying to convince

Nelson to speak in unison with him, although marginalization seemed to help Nelson voice his disagreement. In essence, Branscomb hoped that Nelson might save the chancellor's reputation over the fallout for the expulsion, just as Nelson had hoped Lawson's voluntary withdrawal might limit the damage from the act.[38]

Instead, public support buoyed Nelson while further enraging Branscomb. Guest speakers Liston Pope, dean of Yale Divinity School, his colleague Roland H. Bainton, and L. Harold DeWolf from Boston University (the latter only five years removed from supervising Martin Luther King Jr.'s doctoral dissertation) visited campus to inaugurate the new Divinity School building. The three used the occasion to condemn Branscomb's acts, which only added to the chancellor's intense displeasure. Said DeWolf, "Jesus, who ate and drank with sinners and paid his tax when it was due, nevertheless violated the law by his technically disorderly conduct as he cleansed the temple in the name of God." DeWolf added that "to demand conformity to an order or culture based on injustice and falsehood is to cry 'peace' where there is no peace." Bainton's lecture also conspicuously needled the chancellor; his talk "traced Christian history showing it was filled with conflicts over the proper speed and manner of achieving social change." Both Boston University and Yale offered Lawson a full scholarship to finish his degree at their universities.[39]

Further rumblings persisted across campus. Although mostly "individual and local," worries about Branscomb's act remained. A few medical school faculty shared misgivings. Another influential figure with similar reservations, physicist Charles Roos, was quietly working on Branscomb. His interest developed after hearing of Lawson's affiliation with the Fellowship of Reconciliation, as his mother was a high-level member as well. After inquiring discreetly with his contacts about Lawson's background, he wrote to Branscomb that the expulsion was a mistake. Branscomb barely engaged with Roos's objections, instead justifying his actions by saying that all he had wanted from Lawson was a promise that the minister "would carry out future protests within the bounds of law." Later Roos reflected that Nelson had erred in soliciting Lawson's lengthy statement of principles, although he did not know that Nelson had tried to streamline this text. What Roos came to realize was that "Harvie needed an ambiguous statement" like "I respect the Constitution as the supreme law of the land." Given the Board of Trust's leanings, that is open to question. But certainly Roos understood the issue more in terms of Branscomb's mismanagement of a fraught dilemma rather than Lawson's moral stance.

Roos, in response, noted to Branscomb that a settlement would allow Vanderbilt "an opportunity to recover its position" and delicately pointed out that perhaps Nelson had taken Branscomb at "face value" when the chancellor asked Lawson for a "strong statement which emphasized his respect for law." Even as the Divinity School faculty remained in the media glare, Roos's role would be central in coming days.[40]

Nonetheless it was here that issues diverged. The racial and activist context for Lawson's dismissal, and the belated consternation of his professors, rapidly became subsumed by internal Vanderbilt politicking. On March 26, Divinity professors Lou Silberman and James Sellers had the first of three conversations with Branscomb exploring the possibility of a compromise over Lawson. These consultations built upon extensive back-channel discussions between the tenth and twentieth of March with Branscomb's administrative team. The Divinity School representatives argued that the South faced a shift in race relations: economic clout and educational advancement had given the African American "new freedom to work for his rights," coupled with Christianity's "spiritual foundation for his efforts." They further suggested that Christian-oriented leadership should be encouraged, "with constructive guidance," to avoid a situation where "despair and impatience may rule" or worse, create a "breakdown of confidence in the constitutional methods." They also asked for a "friendly and forthright discussion" about the regrettable "breakdown of communication" between the Divinity School and the chancellor.[41]

One of Branscomb's assistants had mulled aloud two possibilities: either that Lawson be granted a degree in absentia or that he enroll in Scarritt College. The latter preserved his eligibility for Vanderbilt coursework, thanks to the shared arrangement between the two schools that had already fostered early desegregation at Vanderbilt. Branscomb rejected both ideas, on the grounds that neither would be approved by the board, and on March 30 released a two-page justification for the university's stance on Lawson. The official statement, kept as the sole document for inquiries on the matter, suggested that Vanderbilt had requested that Lawson "agree to confine his activities within legal bounds." When confronted with the panty raid regulation directly, the statement asserted, Lawson had refused "on the grounds of his own view of the usefulness of civil disobedience." Branscomb's statement specified that this was not an issue about freedom of speech, which they would have "gladly defended," but stressed instead that "the university could not sanction nor identify itself with an announced program of deliberate violation of law."[42]

Despite Branscomb's intransigence, the Divinity professors continued dialoguing in part because of sympathetic ears. One journalist wrote privately that "Lawson would like to get back in Vanderbilt . . . and privately Vanderbilt people say they would like to have him back. It could be, however, Vanderbilt has gone so far there is no way to let him back and save face, and it appears unlikely Vanderbilt will permit him back unless some face-saving device can be devised."[43]

The problem was that all efforts to resolve this impasse only worsened the situation. Even normal academic protocols became plotted out in relation to the Lawson case. Thus began an elaborate sequence whereby the Divinity School faculty tried to press the point and the administration resisted them. The combination antagonized both factions even as dialogue continued.[44]

The attempted dissuasions took many different forms. For instance, in early May, the chancellor met with the entire Divinity School faculty and proffered a charm offensive. He told the faculty that they were reminiscent of The Fugitives literary group and confided that he knew that taking the Lawson case directly to the Executive Committee had been a mistake. But, in the meantime, a task force known as the Beach Committee, named after a trusted Branscomb adviser, had been directed to formulate new procedures for future situations such as Lawson's. Branscomb argued that the committee's findings would ensure that such incidents would never be repeated. Moreover, he maintained an inflexible view toward Lawson himself. Indeed, throughout the entire affair, Branscomb refused to talk to Lawson directly. Historian Paul Conkin understood Branscomb's choice as consciously avoiding the risk of having his words used against him, although that is a vexing irony given how exactly that had happened to Lawson. The faculty found themselves particularly puzzled when Branscomb said, "Gentlemen, you shall have your scapegoat. I am willing to resign and announce it immediately effective September 1961"—which they declined because they had no desire for a scapegoat. Although inconclusive, one faculty member wrote that they "went out of that meeting feeling pretty well convinced of the Chancellor's logic and feeling somewhat admiration and sympathy for him caught between us and the B[oar]d of Trust." Indeed, "most of us were convinced of the Chancellor's basic integrity" despite being aware that they would have to make peace with their troubled consciences if the injustice to Lawson remained unresolved. They took for granted Branscomb's advice that it would be impossible to change the board's collective mind.[45]

Still, the professors had been exploring other avenues. One issue concerned the faculty's formal March 8 request asking Branscomb to review the Lawson situation, take it to the full Board of Trust at its next May 21 meeting, and consider a reinstatement. In private conversations, however, Branscomb remained consistently negative about this. He suggested that repeated consultations with trustees showed little inclination to reverse the expulsion. So when Nelson received a letter from Harold S. Vanderbilt on March 17, inviting the Divinity School to attend the May meeting and make their case, the response was one of "dismay." That was Branscomb's job, not theirs, and even after more conversations, the chancellor remained "unyielding" in the opinion that "such a discussion would be most trying and perhaps disastrous."[46]

Meanwhile, Nelson had sounded out Cecil Sims on April 22. The attorney suggested instead that the Lawson issue be removed from the May 21 Board of Trust meeting agenda. Sims counseled that, once the Beach Committee procedures were in place, the terrain might shift enough to readmit Lawson in the summer. Nelson liked that idea and, being in New York City on other business, asked Branscomb's permission to confer with Harold S. Vanderbilt. The chancellor's response was a cool assent, but the instance would later be used against Nelson, portrayed as a "back-run" around Branscomb and grounds for dismissal. In the meeting, Nelson tried to explain the Divinity School position but, given everyone advising against their gambit, formally withdrew the request to the trustees on May 19.[47]

This effort failed both strategically and politically. At an alumni luncheon (the same weekend when visiting speakers roasted Branscomb publicly during the chapel dedication), Nelson conveyed a simple factual overview of the situation to his audience despite Branscomb asking him not to discuss it all. But then a colleague prompted Nelson to speak about Vanderbilt's invitation. The ensuing conversation persuaded the alumni to approve and publicize a resolution advocating for Lawson's reinstatement. This made the newspapers before Nelson could warn Branscomb. In response, Branscomb immediately released a copy of Vanderbilt's letter alongside the information that the Divinity faculty had already withdrawn their request. The effect painted the Divinity School as stubbornly refusing to engage in dialogue with the administration. And it gave Branscomb another reason to impugn Nelson's leadership.[48]

In the meantime, however, Nelson had more pressing matters to deal with, as he had failed to realize how far adrift his colleagues had moved from him. Grumblings about Nelson's handling of Lawson's expulsion had surfaced almost immediately. Even by March 18, not even two weeks after Lawson's arrest, an internal memorandum strongly advised that an outing take place to mend relationships. Professor Arthur Foster, who maintained a running chronology of events throughout the crisis, noted that a "deep breach" within the faculty was apparent based on colleagues disappointed with Nelson's "failure to give strong leadership."[49]

Moreover, Nelson had encouraged other Divinity School members to maintain open lines of communication with administrative officials. He deemed this prudent given Branscomb's new frigidity but also felt guilty about not keeping his colleagues fully informed in early March. That was a mistake. Since he left the details of his colleagues' conversations with university officials to them, it wasn't until May 1 that he realized that the "administration was telling them how I had let them down before the board on March 2, had failed to represent Lawson well, and how I had generally done poor work as a dean." The faculty were now conflicted, unwilling to have Nelson represent them in negotiations yet remaining acutely wary about Branscomb's attempt to scapegoat Nelson. Some contemporaries claimed that underlying resentments about Nelson had been in place long before the Lawson Affair. One person asserted that most colleagues felt that Nelson "didn't understand people or know how to listen." Others refuted this notion strongly and suggested that personal agendas were at play, including from at least one colleague who had unsuccessfully applied for Nelson's job. Nelson retrospectively argued strenuously that he'd had nothing but accolades (both verbal and in the form of pay raises) from Branscomb before this crisis erupted, although he was silent about his colleagues.[50]

At one point, some professors took Nelson aside to warn him about the discontent. But Nelson was disbelieving, seeing this instead as a power play from specific colleagues rather than a general sentiment. So further meetings about the Lawson case continued without the dean present. In Foster's estimation, "there were emerging various centers of power and various informal committees were meeting on their own from time to time, often without consultation with other faculty members." The result was a "sense of uncertainty and perhaps even of distrust." When Nelson found out, he was hurt and paranoid. This prompted Foster, who had never been comfortable with shutting Nelson out, to have an impromptu heart to heart with him. Foster highlighted the impossibility of the situation, given that Nelson had lost the confidence of his colleagues while Branscomb was clearly only biding his time before removing him. The only sound option for Nelson, in Foster's view, was to use the Lawson case as the basis for resigning and "go out a hero." Nelson's response in thanking Foster was that all this was not necessarily news, but "it was simply that he knew it more clearly and unmistakably now."[51]

Events seemed mired in stalemate, presumably just as Branscomb preferred. But then a singular achievement off campus changed the context entirely. The Nashville Movement had continued the sit-ins alongside sustained diplomacy. An explosion rocked Nashville in the early morning hours of April 19 when dynamite was thrown into NAACP lawyer Z. Alexander Looby's house. In response, thousands of Black Nashvillians silently marched through downtown Nashville. The scene culminated in another iconic moment when, under skillful verbal interrogation from student leader Diane Nash, Mayor West publicly conceded that he thought the lunch counters should open to all. On May 10, the stores did so, smoothly and without incident.

The result renewed the Divinity School faculty's energies. Since the desegregation agreement dropped all charges against those who had sat-in, surely, the faculty thought, a new logic must apply to James Lawson. How could his expulsion for civil disobedience be maintained when no prosecutions would happen? As such, professors Sellers and Silberman proposed "the doctrine of magnanimity," which suggested "that a university dare not be less generous than the merchants of Nashville" and thus should "rectify the injustice" to Lawson. Apparently, Branscomb's soundings of board members about this remained negative, and indeed discussion of the Lawson case at the May 21 board meeting supported the chancellor's stance. However, ever since the aborted appeal to the Board of Trust, the Divinity faculty's minds had continued churning. In particular, thoughts kept returning to a March 15 University Senate meeting. Here, Branscomb stated that normal channels were the only appropriate way for Lawson to be welcomed back to Vanderbilt. The chancellor said this because he was keen to disaggregate Lawson's case from the Beach Committee, which had issued genuinely strong protocols protecting academic freedom on campus; he was worried about attempts to apply those retroactively to Lawson's case. Indeed, he deliberately slow-played administrative approval of the Beach Committee report since those conclusions would only starkly show how differently the Lawson case had been handled. But the faculty thought the chancellor's specific wording left some room for appeal. And so the idea of asking Lawson to reapply for admission was born. It seemed tactically clever: Branscomb could blame the Divinity School for readmitting Lawson but argue that blocking this decision would only create more unfavorable publicity. Of course, it would also leave the faculty ostracized if Branscomb took offense. The faculty still hoped that the basic notion that a department should be permitted to admit its own students, particularly now that the legal landscape regarding the sit-ins had changed, would make the chancellor rethink his position.[52]

Yet even with these ongoing efforts, internal anguish within the Divinity School reached a crescendo. Nelson, finally grasping the depth of feeling against him, had hurriedly been doing weeks of urgent shuttle diplomacy. He later claimed that, in these conversations, all the explanations for the discord remained "vague and evasive," but still the "brokenness was obvious." An additional series of "very stormy" group discussions took place. One colleague left in "apparent disgust and anger." Others were embarrassed by the impression that they were trying to backstab Nelson. A "heated argument" took place between two professors. Finally, Nelson commandeered a faculty meeting. There he hurled a blunt account of his work on Lawson's behalf and representing the faculty, trying to rewrite the narrative pinned to him. He accused his colleagues of accepting a "neatly wrapped package labelled 'Nelson's betrayal of the faculty,' which some of you have received so willingly and thankfully from the Chancellor's hand." He decried his own mistakes in giving "free rein to those who felt outraged by the Lawson dismissal and who felt impelled to help rectify it." He rejected being branded as naïve by saying, "it surely wasn't naïve to expect love and trust from colleagues on a theological faculty." His mistake was erroneously believing in a "common good" among his colleagues.

The reaction was severe: hurt feelings mixed with bitterness and indignation. At one point, a faculty member "began to weep and then left." School relationships were now frayed beyond repair. The other theologians agonized over Nelson's place in the school, worrying about whether he should continue as dean and pondering how much that issue was intertwined with Lawson. But their unease only deepened after one consulted with a Branscomb deputy. The message was that any notion of the chancellor's disenchantment with Nelson was false; the dean would be removed only upon the request of his colleagues. This had an even more "demoralizing effect," as the faculty became suspicious that they were falling prey to, as they put it, a divide-and-conquer strategy originating from the administration's offices in Kirkland Hall.[53]

By this point, the Divinity faculty and particularly the admissions committee had only their penultimate gambit. In Nelson's estimation, his colleagues "seemed to look to me now for initiative, and I took it," even though he feared a trap. Many of the past week's meetings had included members of the medical school and other departments. They voiced strong support for the Divinity School and reiterated their willingness to resign if a satisfactory resolution remained elusive. They urged the Divinity School to pursue the possibility of readmitting Lawson.[54]

On May 26, Nelson met Branscomb with the news that the Divinity School had recommended Lawson's readmission for summer term. Nelson requested a quick response because Lawson was simultaneously considering an offer from Boston University. The chancellor was "plainly uncomfortable and irked by this turn of events." Nelson thought that Branscomb had presumed that Divinity School divisiveness would keep Lawson's case buried. Instead the Divinity professors had colleagues foreshadow the move by telling Branscomb that the option was under discussion. The chancellor was annoyed because the glowing character references and the letters of support that he had received publicly and privately did not understand the "real issue," he claimed. Plus he interpreted the insistence on a quick decision as an ultimatum. Nelson explained that this was instead meant to bring clarity for Lawson's choice of next options. He presented the chancellor with a dossier, which included a new statement from Lawson clarifying his views on civil disobedience and nonviolence and affirming that he had always stood for fidelity to the law. Plus Lawson declared that he had resigned from the Fellowship of Reconciliation to focus on writing and pastoral work over the summer and would not be involved in civil rights activity.

Angered by the issue resurfacing, Branscomb ignored the new documentation and the argument that the newly desegregated lunch counters should prompt his reconsideration. Instead, he expressed annoyance with the Divinity School, criticizing Nelson's leadership, the "ungratefulness" of the faculty despite the grant money flowing into their school, and the attitude of a Divinity School that he deemed as "arrogant, self-appointed arbiters of morality for the university." Nelson responded simply that segregation was the chief moral issue of the day and the faculty was compelled to act with Christian witness and "to stake our careers upon our convictions." But he noted that Branscomb continued talking in terms of civil disobedience and Lawson being "thoroughly disruptive of the social order, constitutional government, etc." That the sit-ins had been vindicated remained completely unacknowledged and, while Branscomb trumpeted more recent positive developments for race relations on campus, Nelson kept trying to highlight the specific injustice done to Lawson personally.[55]

During the weekend of Vanderbilt's graduation ceremonies, Nelson felt quietly elated as "congeniality flowed." He noted that Harold S. Vanderbilt and other board members made sure to "greet me with a smile and warm words." The welcomed "sudden, inexplicable show of friendliness led me to think that a happy settlement had actually been decided on."[56]

It was not to be. On May 30, calling the Divinity School admissions committee to his office, Branscomb rejected the attempt to readmit Lawson. In an "angry and insulting" reading of a statement, the chancellor accused the faculty members of being "publicity-seekers" and of acting "with impropriety" in encouraging criticism of Branscomb. He scolded Nelson for meeting with Harold S. Vanderbilt, implying it was against his "wishes" and "advice." He also accused them of falsifying Lawson's grades. Nelson explained privately to a friend that Lawson had had two incompletes in February but made them up and achieved two A minuses. But, after Lawson's dismissal, the Vanderbilt registrar "who constantly worked and informed against us" changed them to Fs. Nelson also claimed that, when the faculty changed them back, they notified Branscomb. The chancellor also chastised the faculty for requesting Lawson's readmission despite declining to appear before the Board of Trust to present their case (even though the latter decision, of course, had been advised by both Sims and Branscomb).

The stunned faculty members felt "pistol-whipped." They realized that Branscomb had played them. He had delayed his response to avoid having potential protests, or a possible public resignation from Nelson, disrupt graduation ceremonies. They also noted the chancellor's contradictory stance in calling the new evidence in the dossier "unconvincing" even as he praised Lawson's remarks on civil disobedience and declared that Lawson's personal statement would have kept the initial expulsion from happening. Now, however, Branscomb thought Lawson should complete his degree in Boston, for the student's return to Vanderbilt "would only insure continuance of conflict on campus."[57]

As word spread, moods were grim. The ugly racial incident had now fully mushroomed into broader issues about academic governance. Nelson later reflected that, despite Branscomb's reputation as "a shrewd politician in Nashville," the chancellor "made a grave tactical error that day," because all four members of the admissions committee witnessed the dressing-down. ("Twice as many witnesses as needed in Judaic law!" Nelson observed wryly.) At an afternoon faculty meeting, Nelson unexpectedly announced his resignation. The move garnered some warm support from his colleagues; at least one saw a marked change toward decisive strength from Nelson since the airing of faculty grievances.[58]

On May 30, nine faculty members agreed to follow through with their planned response if readmission was rejected. They issued their resignations effective August 31, 1960. The delayed date was meant to help their seniors and graduate students finish their respective projects. Rapid-fire developments followed: a colleague with a visiting professorship in Utrecht telephoned in his resignation too, fourteen students withdrew, and three graduates mailed back their diplomas. It was a disastrous look for the university, as journalists rushed to renew the headlines over the dissent. Even worse, the coverage did little justice to the range of issues at stake. One faculty member described the unease as new job offers and telegrams of congratulations "poured in from all over the country," yet "none of us on the faculty felt like heroes." They knew that they had bent over backward for compromise and yet to no avail.[59] The turmoil portrayed in those headlines actually went deeper than most everyone knew, and those uncertainties soon worsened.

3

Endgames and Legacies

GLOOM REIGNED OVER Vanderbilt's campus as summer continued. Unresolved tensions made for rampant disquiet. Events had snowballed away from the injustice done to James Lawson and what that represented for the Black Freedom Struggle. Yet this internal political clash still mattered, symbolically and substantively, in determining what a university should be, how it should be run, and for whom.

The news of the resignations splashed across newspapers and periodicals mangled those issues by mashing information and disinformation. Still, the optics for the university were ugly enough to prompt a flustered response from the chancellor, one that only drove the situation further into morass. Branscomb immediately cornered incoming new hire Walter Harrelson and offered him the deanship of the Divinity School. This was a fraught development for all involved. The faculty was on edge about what would happen to the Divinity School. They were also "unnerved" by the administration's "pressure campaign" haranguing them for meetings and dispatching intermediaries who attempted to change their minds. Harrelson, for his part, was conflicted, not only because of his friendship with Nelson, but also because other colleagues were shaming him for even considering working at Vanderbilt. Nelson, fretting about potential outcomes that might further sideline him, still held out the dim hope that he could preserve his deanship. An awkward miscommunication from his colleagues did not help. In trying to clue him in that remaining as dean was improbable, they failed to adequately convey their real message that they supported him continuing on as a professor. This sent Nelson into a spiral. In the absence of developments, he took to prowling by car around colleagues' houses late at night, looking for proof of conspiratorial meetings, and quizzing people about their whereabouts when they missed his phone calls.[1]

On June 3, the Executive Committee announced that Nelson's resignation was accepted and that the deanship had been offered to Harrelson, who was mulling his decision. No action was taken on the other resignations, which prompted the professors to release their own statement criticizing the attempt to disassociate Nelson from the faculty and thus scapegoat him for the Lawson Affair. In consulting with the Divinity School faculty, Harrelson revealed that he would only accept the deanship if the resigning professors were retained. He asked them what terms would be sufficient for them to stay. The answer was reinstating Nelson as professor and readmitting Lawson. Branscomb, presumably gritting his teeth, acquiesced to the former, but said he could only recommend an in absentia degree for Lawson, based on transfer credits from Boston University, with no guarantee that the board would approve it.[2]

Even as the tug-of-war continued, Branscomb continued trying to steer public perception. The Divinity School carefully kept one copy of the conditions mandated by Harrelson under lock and key and used the only other copy to communicate to the administration. The following day, the full contents ran in the Nashville *Tennessean*.[3]

But the more explosive moment was June 7, when "all hell broke loose." That morning, the Divinity faculty rejected, in turn, meetings requested by both Branscomb and Harold S. Vanderbilt, on the logic that there was nothing to say in the absence of a concrete counteroffer regarding Lawson's readmission. Harrelson had been zigzagging back and forth between Kirkland Hall and the assembled faculty. But finally he announced that Branscomb was holding firm and thus he resigned a professorship never begun (although he would later change his mind).[4]

At a hastily called meeting for all Vanderbilt faculty that afternoon, the Divinity professors watched aghast as Branscomb presented a partisan summary of the situation, in which "familiar charges were paraded in a quite clever manner" in a "purposeful humiliation" of the professors. They now understood their refusal to meet earlier as correct "on principle" but also a "serious strategic error," as Branscomb "made us look very bad indeed, as unreasonable men who would not even discuss with him and Mr. Vanderbilt our differences." At one point, the chancellor criticized the professors for rejecting the attempt to get Lawson a degree via transfer credits. No mention was made that Branscomb himself had advised that this was unlikely to pass the Board of Trust. An account claimed that the Divinity School was "booed" and "hissed" at by colleagues, marking what one professor called their lowest moment, in terms of morale, despite months of turmoil. They were "degraded and dishonored before the whole University faculty," with no acknowledgment of their extensive willingness to negotiate and find common ground. Nelson responded with a brief statement that barely countered the onslaught, insisting that their resignations resulted from the "unfounded" reasons justifying Lawson's expulsion, the "unyielding" negotiations from the administration, and the insufficiency of only recommending an in absentia degree for Lawson. In response, Harold S. Vanderbilt stood to note that he had never witnessed any Vanderbilt chancellor's recommendation be rejected. This point would soon become important.[5]

The turbulent meeting showcased the deadlock. At this point, every overture from either side had failed to register. One person recalled how faculty representatives at one point went to Belle Meade to meet with some trustees, who greeted them politely with bourbon on the porch. Carefully the professors built their case for an honorable resolution. One suggested that the bad publicity would mar Vanderbilt's good name for decades and the school would "cease to be a major university." If "no one will consider coming here," Vanderbilt would have the reputation of being merely "a Southern finishing school." The response was, "Well, sir, we'll take the Southern finishing school."[6]

But, more slowly, support for the Divinity School surfaced. On June 8, Silberman spoke to an American Association of University Professors (AAUP) meeting on campus with some 150 professors in attendance, explaining the Divinity School faculty's position more clearly and finding widespread backing. "It was an angry meeting," Nelson later recorded; resentment toward Branscomb and the board was intense. Some called for resignations on the spot. One person declared "that this was the first time all spring they had been able to hear our side of the story." The flabbergasted Divinity professors also learned the extent of false rumors present, including, for example, one that they had rejected the use of an outside mediator. They were becoming aware of how little they had shaped the discourse about these issues except in their own conversational bubbles.[7]

This growing backing changed the negotiations. Pockets of influential allies helped, present in all departments but most critically in the School of Medicine—the crown jewel of Vanderbilt University and recipient of multimillion dollar grants. The volume of support at the AAUP meeting paralleled a stinging newspaper article. Written by a *Tennessean* reporter, but rejected by his local editor before being published by the *New York Herald Tribune*, the story wondered if Vanderbilt was about to "become a mockery of the word university itself." Internal dissent and external ridicule now combined powerfully. Campus sentiment to curtail the Board of Trust's power swelled. Some medical faculty members had submitted resignations in support of the Divinity School, a development that the university was frantically trying to keep hushed and in abeyance. By one account, seven million dollars in research funding was at stake; this made Branscomb immediately call the Divinity School. Figures in the medical school also facilitated a "frank and friendly discussion" between the aggrieved Divinity scholars and Harold S. Vanderbilt, who defended Branscomb but seemed to appreciate the professors' position.[8]

Vanderbilt's increased role resulted directly from physicist Charles Roos's quiet lobbying behind the scenes. Increasingly troubled by the ongoing crisis, Roos also grappled with a "real moral dilemma." He had no worries for his own situation. Nor was he especially invested in Lawson in particular. But he was acutely aware that further resignations would spell "the end of any significant University growth for probably ten years." His revelation was sudden, as he later told the story: he realized "Branscomb was concerned about showing that he was in charge . . . I had been wasting my time arguing Jim Lawson's case; this was really about administrative power."[9]

So Roos concentrated on the one person who could end the stalemate: Harold S. Vanderbilt. Meeting with Vanderbilt and Branscomb, he showed them the *Tennessean*'s front page, which had printed two contrasting photos: a happy Lawson at Boston University (BU) beside a more dour one at Vanderbilt. "Who is running this University?" he asked, and turned the screw by noting that the image was "not the kind of picture you wanted published at a time of social tension." He then announced his intent to "resign with regret," plus his recent meeting with nearly twenty like-minded colleagues. He estimated that another round of resignations would be a major setback for the school. He later explained that the statement was intended less for Branscomb, whom he knew would not be threatened and gave a "snotty" reaction, but more for Harold S. Vanderbilt: "we looked each other in the eye for what seemed like forever, but was about twenty seconds."

From then on, Vanderbilt was in charge. In Roos's appraisal, Vanderbilt thought Stahlman and Sloan were the problem: "To him it was a ridiculous situation." But only Vanderbilt could cajole Branscomb toward a resolution. In subsequent meetings, Roos observed how Vanderbilt would criticize Roos's arguments and then propose something substantively the same: "It was clearly for Harvie's benefit." When Branscomb complained that Lawson had upset the chancellor's internal timetable for desegregating, Roos remembered Vanderbilt soothingly saying, "Harvie, I think you would have done the same thing," which completely deflated Branscomb's resistance. And yet, Branscomb's real stubbornness was over Nelson, not Lawson. "We spent eight hours together, the three of us, only," Roos remembered. "I had Lawson back in thirty minutes. The rest of the time was what we did with Nelson."[10]

Roos approached the Divinity professors after their presentation at the AAUP meeting. He, with Harold S. Vanderbilt's help, had set aside the issue of Lawson's and Nelson's real or perceived motivations and convinced Branscomb that, regardless of extraneous events, the chancellor had the right to choose his deans and the Divinity faculty their students. The physicist's instructions were that "Lawson could have his VU degree if the DSF [Divinity School faculty] could find any way for him to earn it that had not been publicly rejected." Roos showed them a document, dictated but not signed by Branscomb. It stated that, when the Divinity faculty decided Lawson had met the requirements for graduation, Branscomb would endorse the decision and, if the board refused, he would resign.[11]

After conferring, the faculty agreed on the essential condition that Lawson be allowed back on campus. One of the professors came up with an idea: giving Lawson individual tutorials to finish his spring semester work would permit him to graduate without attending classes. Both could claim victory: the school would say Lawson was merely completing his coursework; the administration could similarly argue that the restriction against further attendance had been maintained. Various discussions continued throughout the night and following day between Branscomb, Vanderbilt, Silberman, and Roos. At one point, Roos later recalled, one of Branscomb's assistants tried to shame the Divinity faculty for disloyalty. This prompted Silberman to speak "for fifteen minutes on the obligation of the University faculties to seek TRUTH and the real meaning of academic freedom." It was, Roos wrote, "the most eloquent speech I have ever heard and I wished at the time it had been recorded. When Lou finished there was complete silence for almost a minute." After hours of nitpicking over words and details, finally Vanderbilt asserted, "This is not a proposal, this is agreed. Can you get agreement from your faculty?" With Lawson's approval, it was done.[12]

Or so everyone thought. The relieved professors believed that their cause was won. Nelson remained the problem. He knew his position was untenable. Branscomb had agreed with Roos (at the direction of Harold S. Vanderbilt) that Nelson would resign as dean, but with an additional year of employment to look for another job with the university's assistance. But Roos did not know about the breach between Nelson and his faculty. Plus Nelson distrusted Branscomb intensely at this point and feared a broken promise. He requested instead that his offer to resign be declined, so that he would still be dean when the compromise was reached, but pledged in writing to resign twenty-four hours later. This arrangement, he felt, would vindicate his own honor, and he claimed that Lawson would reject the terms if Nelson ended up blamed for the entire affair. The written assurance protected Branscomb from the possibility of Nelson reneging while serving as insurance against Nelson's suspicion that Branscomb was not "acting in good faith." This was also agreed. With that, at long last, a sense of exhilaration and relief descended, all the sweeter after months of unknowns.[13]

Then, a new crushing bombshell, the "big betrayal": The Executive Committee rejected this arrangement despite Branscomb's recommendation—and thus established the first exception to the precedent that Harold Vanderbilt had publicly declared as ironclad. It also contradicted the Executive Committee's own June 7 statement clearing Branscomb to resolve the situation however the chancellor saw fit. The resultant recriminations were ugly. Nelson felt vindicated in mistrusting Branscomb; Roos tried to convey that Branscomb and Vanderbilt had been supportive but had been overruled by the Executive Committee. The faculty publicly released Branscomb's letter offering to resign if the proposal was rejected (which they later allowed might have been a mistake); the chancellor responded tellingly that "I have made no such statement for publication." Lou Silberman countered that the negotiators "went over it word for word." Said his colleague Arthur Foster wearily, "I think the Executive Committee is playing with us like a yo-yo."[14]

Although perplexed and perturbed by developments, Roos decided that, rather than wring his hands, "I was going to write the headlines." By the following day, 161 Vanderbilt faculty members had on short notice signed a petition denouncing the board. Roos made sure that the wording was framed as "supporting Chancellor Branscomb in his fight with the Board of Trust" to foreground the issue of academic governance. Reports circulated that a significant medical school contingent had resigned. The mood on campus was worse than ever. Silberman stated, "I cannot go through another single day of negotiations. Today was the most humiliating day in my life. Today I became an old man." He added that, "I, for the first time and last time in my life, was dealing in human flesh—namely, Bob Nelson." Two days later, Harold S. Vanderbilt was admitted to hospital with heart trouble. At this point Nelson commented to friends that "there was no longer any moral justification" for a divinity school at Vanderbilt, as it had "no autonomy" nor any "protectors in high places."[15]

As ever, key issues were not as reported. The supposed sticking point was Branscomb's unwillingness "to let Nelson go out on his own terms," as one faculty member saw it. Silberman told Nelson that "the chancellor hates you with a hate which passes all understanding." But this was another public relations dodge. Branscomb blaming Nelson misdirected focus from the core issue that the chancellor had been overruled by his own board. Despite sniffing that Nelson's request was "more for propaganda purposes" than a real solution, Branscomb had previously agreed to the terms, as Roos confirmed. The Executive Committee's declaration that it would only negotiate over a possible in absentia degree for Lawson was similarly curious. This solution had been discussed long ago but rejected by Branscomb because he felt it would not pass the board. Silberman also noted that the Divinity School might have found this at least a good starting point for negotiations back in early May; indeed, it was the basis for much of the informal conversations between the Divinity School and Branscomb's advisers, but was always set aside.[16]

Behind the headlines, the realities emerged more slowly among those in the know. The fuss over Nelson's resignation conveniently distracted from the more damaging reality: the wholesale willingness of the Executive Committee's more reactionary members to purge the dissenting faculty. Weeks later, James Stahlman took umbrage at Branscomb's smokescreen about Nelson, arguing that the committee was mostly willing to accept Lawson's in absentia degree but could not condone the resigning faculty's return. Stahlman also disclosed that Harold S. Vanderbilt had remained silent about facilitating the Roos proposal and had announced a unanimous rejection of the same even though it was not. Nor did Stahlman know about Branscomb's offer to resign until it was reported in the newspapers.

The import of this is crucial. Aside from his rage at being outflanked, Stahlman's letter suggested that a diploma for Lawson was immaterial compared to the foremost requirements that Lawson not be physically allowed back on campus and the malcontented Divinity faculty be purged. Stahlman's anger toward Harold S. Vanderbilt derived from the latter steering the public image of the Executive Committee acting with one voice even when it was not. Thus Branscomb's and Vanderbilt's dissembling helped obscure the divisions within the board and administration, even though Harold Vanderbilt's stance meant another round of headlines before prevailing.[17]

After all the dissension and upheaval, with all the conniving and planning, the meetings and proposals, the misunderstandings and disinformation—it was over. Boxed in by major pillars of Vanderbilt's recent successes imploding in the Divinity and medical schools, and bypassing alternate proposals from Stahlman and Vanderbilt, Branscomb issued an abrupt June 13 statement that tried to impose closure. With curious logic, he used the sit-ins to justify the expulsion. He claimed that the fact that some thirty white Vanderbilt students participated in the protests without punishment proved the university's principle that "racial progress in the South must be based on obedience to law." Instead, Lawson was singled out because of "his commitment to an active program of civil disobedience." Regardless, "on his own authority as chancellor," he outlined that 1) Nelson's resignation was now accepted, effective immediately; 2) that Lawson could finish his coursework at BU and have the credits transferred to VU, or without reenrolling take written exams to finish his VU coursework, with either option yielding his degree; 3) that those Divinity faculty who had resigned had ten days to withdraw those resignations; that 4) he now considered the matter fully closed.[18]

Superficially, Branscomb finally caved when he acknowledged that he alone had the ability to readmit a student and did so. As one person remarked later, "I think this made the Board happy because they frankly had the reaction that Branscomb had created the problem in the first place." Branscomb never should have ceded his power of intervention to the Executive Committee. But only protection from Harold S. Vanderbilt allowed the chancellor to stand up to his board and fix the error. As Roos later summed up: Branscomb was "scared of Stahlman . . . he just did not feel he had the power to buck Stahlman. He was trapped, he had seen the collapse of all that he had worked to achieve; he did not see any way out until Harold Vanderbilt began to use his power." And Branscomb "knew he had made a mistake; he as much admitted to me the week after Jim was dismissed."[19]

The Divinity faculty remained underwhelmed by the proposal. They realized that they had failed to prevent Nelson's scapegoating and failed to secure Lawson's return to campus. And they felt like Branscomb's terms required them to "crawl back" and "beg for their jobs." But other Vanderbilt colleagues saw it differently and now put a new pressure campaign upon them to stay. Although they "did not blame us if we all left," Foster wrote, they also said, "with tears in their eyes," that the school was the "soul of the university."[20]

On June 15, the Divinity School faculty withdrew their resignations, except for one who had already procured a job elsewhere. They based their decision on the belief that the situation could be "resolved honorably" and that they had successfully established Lawson's right to earn his degree, even though Lawson eventually opted to stay in Boston. They cautioned that this did not constitute an acceptance of Branscomb's views but rather a choice to reorient toward a longer-term healing of campus rifts. Despite mixed feelings, the consensus was that this was the "most right" option. They added that, although Nelson had "released them from any personal obligations," which he had done only reluctantly, they still disapproved of "the summary dismissal of Dean Nelson" as "unjust and ungracious." In meeting with Branscomb to share the decision, the chancellor said, "Gentlemen, I do not know who founded the Divinity School but tonight you have refounded it." One account said the chancellor "shook hands three times with the men during their brief stay, which is some indication of his feeling at the time." As the dust settled, Nelson took a temporary position at Princeton and later joined the faculty at Boston University. The three Black Divinity students also re-enrolled at Vanderbilt.[21]

Other responses were stinging. Nelson was pilloried within the white Nashville community. One member of West End Methodist Church not only scorned both Kasper and Lawson as "carpetbaggers" but wrote that he "deplore[d] your melodramatic and adolescent resignation" and that "our rather conservative community and our cherished school," whether "right or wrong," would "rather preserve domestic tranquility than incite riot and civil commotion over your petty squabbles." Others, writing that Nelson had "tried to destroy a great institution which we hold very close to our hearts," decried the sit-ins and the notion that "Jesus' command to turn the other cheek" had anything to do with those protests: "the breaking of laws for material and personal gain."[22]

Some civil rights leaders in Nashville were also disappointed for diametrically opposite reasons and let the theologians know it—C. T. Vivian in particular, although Andrew White and white civil rights supporter

Will D. Campbell were more sanguine. Vivian's *Nashville News Star* editorially decried Nelson's scapegoating (he was "more wronged than wrong") and castigated Branscomb "whose pride has become more important than the character and reputation of men of honor, to admit, by their actions or by their words, that they are wrong." The paper quoted Reverend J. C. Copeland that "Nashville is a modern day Ninevah now," and that "she has sat down in sackcloth and ashes. Everybody from the highest political office to the least person has repented, except Chancellor Branscomb." Similarly, Everett Tilson's consistent disgust with colleagues even after moving out of state solidified an estrangement with his colleagues that never healed.[23]

A week later, the Divinity professors and Lawson held an extensive debriefing. The faculty sensed that Tilson had been actively campaigning for media figures to suggest that Lawson's return to Vanderbilt would be a grave whitewashing of what had occurred. And they knew that Lawson and Nelson had been in contact. They still hoped that Lawson would honor the agreement and underline the episode as a victory. Lawson remained unsure, and the discussion underscored the decided haziness of the resolution. Lawson understood that Nelson's return to Vanderbilt was functionally impossible but noted that their legacies were now intertwined. "Nelson's departure and my expulsion are of the same kind," he had insisted publicly. "I think what the university has done [represents] the church defeated, church at its worst" while "Dean Nelson is the church victorious and triumphant." The professors thought Lawson "had a pretty realistic picture of all the persons and events involved." They appreciated him not being judgmental about their decision. He did opine that the settlement "had indeed compromised principle" by solidifying Nelson's image as a scapegoat, which he found unacceptable. He was also conscious that the atmosphere on campus remained inhospitable for free speech and civil rights activity. While understanding that the Beach Committee had set new protocols in place, and aware of the new "self-discovery of the faculty," he knew his choice not to return matched Stahlman's preferences. Some professors mused how Lawson was now "captive to his public image" in choosing his next steps, not able to act according to "how things are rather than how things look." This was perhaps an indictment of their own position, and certainly a point of broader import for an entire episode where private dialogues and public portrayals were usually at odds.[24]

Stahlman, too, was furious at the outcome. He insisted that Branscomb had expelled Lawson and the Executive Committee had merely ratified the decision. He would have gladly accepted the resignations from both the Divinity and medical schools. In fact, he had, along with fellow trustee O. H. Ingram, proposed doing just that—and had initially resisted Branscomb's belated attempt to take back control when the chancellor did. But even Stahlman's conspiratorial views about the "undermining and divisive tactics" of the Divinity School meant that he had to toe the line once Branscomb, with Harold S. Vanderbilt's tacit support, made his conclusive move. No matter how much ire he vented, he and his beloved university needed Harold S. Vanderbilt too. Stahlman's only recourse was an editorial criticizing Branscomb for not doing what he did earlier. Later he stressed his self-professed "sentimental (at times, call it fanatical, if you will) devotion to Vanderbilt," and resistance to those "dedicated to the venomous task of damaging and if need be, destroying the university." But he also highlighted to Branscomb how much he resented the chancellor's perceived lack of loyalty in "thumbing his nose" at the Executive Committee after they "stood by you when the wolves were howling and nipping at your heels." As always, devotion on his own terms was Stahlman's foremost requirement. He found particularly objectionable Branscomb's threatened resignation that "appeared to me and to others to have been a bit of showmanship for the benefit of the faculty, loyalists and dissidents, as well as for people generally who always admire a display of 'independence.'"[25]

The episode stained Vanderbilt for years. A year's probation from the American Association of Theological Seminaries followed, even as Branscomb sang a more cheerful tune to his outside funders. In a report to the Ford Foundation, he dismissed "the easy impression that Vanderbilt is a reactionary Southern institution." He stressed instead how the publicity showed that "we do admit Negro students" and that the university had "proven its ability to handle a serious crisis" with debate. "The issue of one law," he wrote, "which must be accepted in principle for all parties in these tense racial situations when they occur seems established." He added that "we have emerged as the leader of the Southeast in this area of race relations, namely that we are going forward with constructive steps, but do not yield to demands for radical campaigns that cannot be sanctioned or supported by institutions which are largely Southern in constituency, control, and support." It was a desperate attempt to save face—and a successful one, as the grant money continued. One Divinity School member later wrote to Nelson saying that the affair had pushed Vanderbilt in "an integrationist direction," albeit in a cynical way: "We understand that the recent large Ford grant simply would have been out of the picture if we had not returned and if we did not have the good Negro enrollment which we have this year (5 new Negro students, I believe)." He was more correct than he knew. Throughout the entire affair, Charles Roos kept private a detail that he was sworn to secrecy about, that several of the Ford Foundation's trustees were FOR members like Lawson. A lack of resolution to the Lawson case would have doomed funding for years. Branscomb, in private correspondence with the Ford Foundation, promised to fully desegregate Vanderbilt before he retired. Conflict remained necessary to achieve social gains, but Black people at Vanderbilt remained figures used to placate wider audiences, be it sacrificial lambs for segregationists or symbols of progress for funders.[26]

Even as the immediate aftermath slowly waned, the battle over what it all meant continued to be contested ground, fought over in the rewriting of events. Many later attested to how Branscomb "suffered intensely in private" because of the incident. Perhaps this is so. But his response to that inner turmoil was to add self-serving accounts. These showed tangled intellectual contortions, defending his own actions while casting Nelson in the worst possible light. Branscomb highlighted the supposed "difficulties which Dean Nelson was having with his faculty" and Nelson's "own lack of candor in dealing with the officers of the University." He claimed he had specifically asked Nelson if he could be diplomatic when it came to negotiating racial issues on campus, since Nelson was not a Southerner. And he maintained that Nelson perpetuated the Lawson issue so as "to play the role of a valiant protagonist of minority rights and privileges, with the alternatives of winning or of resigning on high moral grounds." This is manifestly not true, given how Nelson was initially too inclined in the reverse direction, trying to keep Lawson in school before yielding to Lawson's principles. But it shows Branscomb's sense of betrayal over Nelson's campaign against the chancellor after the expulsion.

Likewise, Branscomb defended the Executive Committee's decision to reject the Roos compromise because it would "have given [Nelson] a clean bill of health, only to slap the University the following day with another highly publicized resignation and accompanying statement." As Charles Roos observed, Branscomb believed Nelson was using Lawson "to benefit his reputation at the expense of Branscomb and Vanderbilt University." The egoism in Branscomb's perspective found it easier to deride Nelson rather than allow for the chancellor's own mistakes. Still, Nelson's prevarications, both in supporting Lawson and standing up to Branscomb, ended up doing neither effectively; worse, they made Nelson a convenient target for Branscomb to project his own deficiencies upon. The chancellor's rage against the dean surely smoldered hotter as Branscomb's own dependence on Harold Vanderbilt and his impotency against Stahlman became clearer.[27]

The archival record also preserves Nelson's efforts to counter Branscomb's claims. He described how the chancellor thought of him as his "prize catch" and "the conscience of the university" on moral questions, plus conferred with him on administrative matters. While presumably this only enhanced Branscomb's sense of betrayal, Nelson emphasized that Branscomb's disenchantment was falsely concocted only after the Lawson Affair. In correspondence with others, Nelson also stressed Lawson's exemplary record, highlighted Branscomb's misremembering events, and chided Branscomb's reliance on the "panty raid rule." On the latter, Nelson noted that "the dean of men, who drafted the rule last year, told me it was never intended for graduate students nor for anything but prankish misdemeanors." He also quoted with relish evidence of the chancellor's hypocrisy. In 1952, Branscomb had argued that a core contribution of religion in American life was "the insistence upon a law of God which is supreme above all human institutions and man-made legislation" and that laws that "deviate from this standard have no moral authority" and should be "disregarded and rejected."[28]

Branscomb and Nelson later corresponded, as the former dean defended himself while reaching for reconciliation. He reminded Branscomb about the directive for Nelson to be the "moral conscience" of the university and blamed "irreconcilable disagreement" over the "patent" moral issues at stake. The chancellor brushed this aside. To him, the Lawson case was "not over whether certain statutes were legally binding, but on the issue of whether one should obey the law if one did not like it or believe in it." If Lawson "had ever made the statement that he would obey the law as his own attorneys defined it," there would have been no problem. He instead castigated Nelson for being "willing to do anything you could do to wreck the Divinity School" to make his point—an attack that prompted Nelson's confused disbelief. Part of Branscomb's problem was his penchant for quoting Black Nashville lawyer Avon Williams: "We can work within the law and we must work within the law because we are a law-abiding people. These students are law-abiding students, and let's keep it on that plane." As Branscomb later wrote in a public defense of his actions, "that is all we asked of Mr. Lawson." Yet, as Williams protested diplomatically in print, Branscomb had conveniently omitted the preceding sentence where Williams had professed that "the legal and moral issues are exactly the same; and that in my opinion the demonstrations carried on by the students were legal.'" Given that Branscomb had completely reversed Williams's point, the attorney demanded a retraction that never came.[29]

Branscomb's rationalizations aged poorly. Twenty years later, he continued arguing that public knowledge of an "Ohio black man with a penitentiary record, being paid a salary by a northern social agency" and directing "an avowed program of civil disobedience from the Vanderbilt campus" would have wrecked the university's integration plans. His conclusion was that, despite administrative mistakes, "the position taken by the Chancellor's office was morally sound," based on the idea that a "selective obedience to law" can be endorsed by individuals but not institutions.[30]

The need to recast his arguments carefully stretched his logic to the breaking point. He had previously argued that the "great problem" of "making the white South obey the law" meant that Lawson could not turn around and selectively choose his adherence to law. Indeed, Lawson was "wrong in principle" to do so because "he and his defenders furthermore demanded of others that in dealings with him they should obey the laws strictly—he should have justice in the courts, the police should act only within legal bounds, etc. etc." He also consistently refused to equate Lawson with comparative examples such as Christian saints who "acted on their own" as part of "their personal testimony" because "the hope of these protestors was to awaken the conscience of society, not to force their view upon society by a form of coercion, the coercion of disorder through organized mass action." Thus he rejected "the extension of Mr. Lawson's personal conscience to the involvement of complex social institutions" and argued that "the University never questioned Mr. Lawson's right to take the position he announced to the Mayor; it only requested that he withdraw and conduct his program on his own responsibility without involving the university."[31]

The reality remained that Branscomb's arguments were completely bankrupt. He never cited the specific law that Lawson broke—he deferred to West's legal assessment as correct and binding, ignoring that the white hecklers were the real lawbreakers and that all charges against the protestors were dropped in the May 10 settlement. He used an administrative rule spuriously, fabricating an elaborate excuse (much like Ben West fashioned a debatable interpretation of law and a deliberate misunderstanding of Lawson's rhetoric) to justify his chosen preferences. The chancellor applied it wrongly, given that Lawson did not participate in Big Saturday nor involve Vanderbilt University in the sit-ins in any way. He applied it disproportionately, as the fifteen students punished under the rule prior to March 1960 had only been suspended, not expelled. Nor did he apply it to other white students who physically participated in the sit-ins. He also maintained a posture of judicial fidelity even while dispensing with any formal university procedures for Lawson to defend himself and appeal the expulsion. He ignored the recommendations of those who taught Lawson directly without ever meeting Lawson himself. And despite, like West, hoping that the sit-ins would be delayed until the legal issues were resolved, he left himself permission to break laws that he regarded as invalid, as with his act of desegregating Vanderbilt in the first place. The incomprehensible arguments of his retrospective accounts betray him—these were the words of someone agonizingly trying to justify something that they knew would never be vindicated.[32]

Nelson is a more sympathetic figure due to the abuse heaped upon him. The contempt he received was disproportionate to his mistakes. He understood his own errors clearly. He knew he should have rejected from the beginning the logic applying the panty raid rule to Lawson and changed the conversation, including asserting his right as dean to handle the charges against Lawson. But he emphasized later how Branscomb "gave the orders" from the beginning and ignored any contrary ideas. Morally and procedurally, Nelson's efforts to find a middle ground eroded underneath his feet. He realized his emphasis on preserving the Divinity School was misguided compared to the injustice to Lawson. Whatever simmering issues he had with his faculty only boiled over spectacularly because of the Lawson situation. And he misjudged the political climate and how Lawson's expulsion would celebrate the activist and shame the university, rather than the other way around. Many are quick to dismiss him as naïve, lacking administrative nous; Paul Conkin dismisses him as someone trying to impress Branscomb as a father figure. It is hard to know what he should have done when a university chancellor, a mayor, and a prominent newspaper publisher were hell-bent with other ideas. Perhaps his real issue was the delay in finding a firmness of voice and a strength of conscience. His support for integration did not translate to his higher-ups any more than Lawson's did, and the interval cost Nelson dearly as a perceived betrayal rather than appropriate attention to his actual beliefs.[33]

For the Divinity School faculty, the slow awakening over the moral issue quickly folded into cognizance of broader repercussions about academic governance. Their collective and praise-worthy resignations nonetheless are too heroically cast given the range of sentiment and realities behind that stance. Even as they scored some abstract points and rightly highlighted the contradictions in Branscomb's words and deeds, it was literally a different language than the considerations of administrative governance that dictated events. Their willingness to compromise made sense for institutional preservation but complicates their lauded legacy, as they well knew. And only after the crisis widened to include professors from the sciences and medicine did the Divinity School's position have an impact—and highlight the realities of university power. If more resolute in their convictions and willingness to resign, strictly speaking they were only marginally more effective than Nelson despite their criticisms of the dean.[34]

Just like Branscomb, the Divinity School faculty had their own version of retroactive grappling with what the Lawson Affair meant. A number of denominational publications discussed the event, often with essays from Divinity School members wrestling with the moral quandaries therein. Some were conscious about how Vanderbilt's rigidity contrasted with Duke University, for example (which had simply declared that sit-in participants acted as individuals rather than as representatives of the university). So too, they noted how the white elite resistance embodied by the Executive Committee contrasted with "rank and file" reactions in Durham as elsewhere. Vanderbilt Divinity School professor James Sellers, for example, took a moderate tack in being keen to expose the "oversimplification" on both sides, noting the *Banner*'s "fine capacity for arriving easily at pious certitude." Certainly he was not wrong. But, not unlike Branscomb, he remained uneasy with the implications of Lawson's supporters suggesting that everybody working for God was entitled to protection "from the profane powers, such as the Board of Trust, which represent the social order." His opinion was "Nashville has done better than Lawson thinks it has" and claimed instead that Lawson and "his friends, especially professional Northerners, do not seem to understand the tragic depths of the problem of helping white Southerners to see the light." The extent to which Black people needed to be responsible for whites' blindness about racial privilege was one question. So too was the relative emphasis on tragedy when discussing a society based on control and exploitation, as well as the dismissing of Lawson's legal understanding of the sit-ins. The value judgments tangled in those statements remained problematic, as Sellers's former colleague Everett Tilson was quick to pounce on. His essays, by contrast, hammered relentlessly at Vanderbilt's hypocrisy, noting that the university had not been a base of operations for the sit-ins nor had Lawson enjoyed due process to defend himself. "Until Everett Tilson has been denied service at Cross Keys because of his race," he asked rhetorically, "does he have any right to dictate to Negroes the means by which they should seek service at downtown lunch counters?"[35] Especially given, as Tilson might have added, that those means succeeded.

Of course Stahlman and his ilk, in their reactionary efforts, are easy if appropriate villains. Consider how the recalcitrants on the Executive Committee demanded that they get their way only until the costs of doing so became too high and threatened the university itself. Then Stahlman used his column to scold Branscomb for doing precisely the thing to which they had acquiesced. Their emphasis on loyalty actually insisted on like-mindedness. Branscomb himself later surmised that much of the Executive Committee's hard-line sentiment derived from the bitter divorce that Vanderbilt had undergone in 1914 to disassociate from its Methodist origins. Hence some board members, regarding the Divinity School as an "academic embarrassment and a financial burden," preferred to liquidate the school. But he also noted how the board viewed many of the faculty's racial opinions as "moral exhibitionism" rather than genuine interest in integration. Judging the motivations of others was easier than reconsidering one's own opinions. Regardless, the board's treatment both of Lawson and the resigning faculty accentuated how poised it was to police Vanderbilt as a predominantly white space, sealed off from expressions of dissent and with only carefully chosen examples of difference.[36]

Still, Stahlman's example should not obscure the range of white sentiments encompassing people like Cecil Sims or Branscomb. Each deferred to white anxieties and delusions about white supremacy in different ways. That rich array of different submissions to white preferences highlights important historical nuance, consequentially so. Yet, regardless of those differences, these mentalities all helped their institutions perpetuate racial injustice. And that insight should extend to Mayor Ben West, who is uncritically viewed by history as "seeing the light" as the Nashville protestors challenged him in public after the Looby bombing. This interpretation clashes both with his actions to persecute Lawson and later events in his tenure.[37]

Over the next couple years, Vanderbilt nominally surmounted more barriers by phasing in other dimensions of desegregation. Still, racial (and town/gown) issues continued to be a problem for years thereafter.

Whatever Branscomb felt or did privately, his hyper-vigilance against potential incidents led to acts that seemed to suggest tacit agreement with segregationists. In the years following the Lawson Affair, for instance, he publicly endorsed a book by Vanderbilt segregationist Donald Davidson and wrote approving responses to letter-writers advocating racist views. Although abhorrent, one might argue that these were cheap gestures that meant nothing in terms of actual actions; others might highlight that they still had a legitimizing effect, regardless of Branscomb's intent. But he disavowed an interracial conference that occurred on campus without his knowledge. He also scorned a white Vanderbilt professor of physics who had been assaulted while supporting civil rights protests in the city (even as many noted that the positive coverage of that professor, David Kotelchuk, was a welcome rejoinder to the university's lingering reputation after Lawson's expulsion.)

Regardless, Vanderbilt moved slowly toward open admissions despite a mixed reception from different constituencies on campus. The final decision approving this, one historian noted, was "in no sense a vote in favor of significant or full integration" and indeed left ultimate discretion for admission to deans and the chancellor. That proviso was understood as veto power to prevent Black Northerners from enrolling. The first Black undergraduates joined in 1964. The year after, all schools had Black students. And by 1966, the university had begun "actively recruiting" Black students to campus. Charles Roos remembers meeting Branscomb for coffee just days after the final decision to integrate fully was ratified. The chancellor "looked me straight in the eyes and said with a mischievous smile: 'I paid you back.'"[38]

As that process continued, history seemed doomed to eerily repeat when Lawson reapplied for admission at the end of the decade. The dean was Walter Harrelson, who had ended up joining the Divinity School amid the 1960 crisis. Vanderbilt's new chancellor, Alexander Heard, unsure about the terms from 1960, did not know if admission was permissible. It set off another mini-storm of conflicts. The Executive Committee and James Stahlman blocked Lawson's readmission before they were outmaneuvered, in what historian Paul Conkin suggests was the final stand of the old guard controlling Vanderbilt's Board of Trust. Perhaps all too symbolically, it was at a board meeting in 1976 where Stahlman suffered the stroke that would end his life.[39]

Most accounts stress Branscomb's mistakes with the Lawson Affair as a grievous if momentary flaw in judgment and a tragedy given the rest of his career. They cite the immense pressure he labored under and what he accomplished in terms of steering Vanderbilt into a new era. Fuller accounts of the Lawson Affair often end on the same note: in 1996, Branscomb and Lawson had a private meeting where the chancellor verbalized his genuine regret over the mistakes he made. "It was the worst decision I've ever made, and it still troubles me even now," he said. "And I hope you can find it in your heart sometime to forgive me for that." Lawson's response was to take Branscomb by the hand and say, "Dr. Branscomb, I forgave you a long time ago. I never thought you were anything but a Christian gentleman in a very difficult situation. So I have forgiven you, and I want you to know that." It was in keeping with Lawson's theological perspective. "He had by then recognized that he had allowed some things to take a wrong turn in 1960," Lawson said. "My own major reflection as I look back upon it is that we have to accept the man as he was, as we have to accept ourselves, because in the situation we get, we all make errors." Even as some people, even religiously inclined ones, remained skeptical about this moment of Branscomb asking forgiveness after all that had occurred, Lawson noted simply that the affair had evolved to a point far beyond the civil rights movement.[40]

But it is more appropriate to return to Lawson and reclaim the story on his terms. Despite all the fuss, Lawson was relatively untroubled by the expulsion. "I went on with my life," he said, "the movement was the main story." His journey continued, although capturing his subsequent career requires another book. He finished his degree at Boston University. He delivered a keynote lecture at the founding of SNCC and instigated that organization's profession of nonviolence in its founding statement. However tenuously that belief held up across the wider Movement, his example magnified nonviolent possibilities for adherents that never extinguished. The colleagues he trained in Nashville fanned out across the region, each playing instrumental roles in key battlefields of the civil rights movement. Alongside his Nashville brethren, Lawson helped regain the impetus of the Freedom Rides in 1961, propelling them further into the Deep South and heightening their demonstrative power as they continued. He became a pastor at Centenary Methodist Church in Memphis in 1962, fusing together activism widely across racial, labor, and economic issues, including playing a key role in the 1968 sanitation workers' strike. At Lawson's imploring, Martin Luther King came there to lend his voice before being murdered on April 4. In 1974, Lawson moved to Los Angeles as pastor of Holman United Methodist Church and redoubled his advocacy on behalf of workers, race relations, civil liberties, gay and reproductive rights, and pacifist movements locally and internationally. He maintained that he was arrested many more times for supporting labor unions in California than in the South for civil rights causes.[41]

Lawson intensified his relationship with Vanderbilt in later decades before passing away on June 9, 2024. He was named a distinguished alumnus of the university in 1996, despite not being an alumnus, and served as a Distinguished Professor from 2006 to 2009. He donated many of his personal papers to the university archives and had scholarships and professorships established on his behalf. The university also has an institute for the study of nonviolent social movements bearing his name. Few would dispute the worthiness of those honors, nor their appropriateness as redress.

Still, his thoughts from March 1960 are perhaps truer for this particular story, threading through the dense tangle of issues that his presence provoked among white Nashvillians and settling upon simpler and more powerful truths for himself. As David Halberstam, reporter in Nashville during 1960, wrote:

> When the police came and handcuffed him at Kelly Miller Smith's church, Jim Lawson felt a vast sense of relief. For the first time since the entire crisis at Vanderbilt had begun, he felt comfortable with himself. He was tired of being caught in the byzantine politics of a white university. Doing what was right for the Movement and taking great risks for something so basic to his spirit was easy.[42]

Epilogue

THE LAWSON AFFAIR DISTILLED a curious contradiction: that, even as the sit-ins fundamentally rattled perspectives about race relations in 1960, the aftereffects were varied and uncertain. This scale of nonviolent direct action, placing bodies directly in forbidden places, triggered a range of soul-searching about social and cultural norms not easily answered. In terms of the Lawson episode, the word that best characterized the whole situation, according to the consensus of some participants decades later, was *ambiguity*. This holds true, not just for the protagonists, but also for the meanings we try and wrest from this story. We have seen how the legal aspects of the sit-ins showcased particular ambiguities, as did the questions over academic freedom. Lawson's "experiment" with nonviolent direct action certainly qualifies too, as does the theological dimensions of the episode, given how the act of bodily witness and religious messaging from civil rights protestors made many whites ponder whether their beliefs served God or Caesar. Far too many continued to choose the latter, but enough wrestled with the display of commitment from protestors that the fairness of civil rights was talked about differently. Consciousness about these issues changed massively, even if tangible change materialized far more slowly and imperfectly.[1]

Precisely because of all these ambiguities, the conclusions people drew about Lawson's expulsion differ widely. That was true then and remains so today. The crisis was about nonviolent direct action—but also social control. It was about law—but also morality. It was about religion—but also academic politics. It was about institutional structures and academic freedom—but it was also about civil disobedience. It was about James Lawson—but it was also about Vanderbilt as a university community.

Any analysis must allow for all these components to do appropriate justice to this story, what it means and what it may teach us. But, hovering behind all those issues, the Lawson Affair was ultimately about the power to decide who belongs and why.

Conflicts like in 1960, Lawson later stressed, have "explosive qualities that none of could have predicted or understood. So it was trial by experiment, by error, for all of us." That said, he also articulated that his expulsion "became an example in the movement of a person's willingness to pay the price" and thus "strengthened our witness." His stance was vindicated by the Movement itself, by legal rulings, and by history. Across the campus and beyond, the repercussions ranged widely. At Vanderbilt, the Beach Committee made explicit the appropriate processes for dealing with situations similar to what had just transpired. The Faculty Senate was strengthened, by some accounts, too. Both secured a more transparent commitment to academic freedom. That said, anxiety persisted, especially within the Divinity School, in the aftermath of what had happened. Nelson recorded that his secretary was hounded so relentlessly by administrators during these events that she needed a prolonged "emotional convalescence" to recover. Other ripple effects were wider. Across the city, many of the more liberally inclined reporters left the *Tennessean* because of how the newspaper had managed its coverage. But other white organizations in the city seemed willing to more visibly facilitate racial change in Nashville, even as those activists empowered by their work in Nashville left to continue their struggle across the South and across the globe. In one historical twist, four students at Yale Divinity School who staged a solidarity march in support of Lawson in 1960 later became integral faculty at Vanderbilt Divinity School. The transmission of Lawson's message did gain traction in unexpected ways, even when religious morality often struggled to facilitate truer integration.[2]

Although the US Supreme Court demurred from addressing the more consequential legal ramifications of the sit-ins, the lower courts fundamentally upheld everyone's right to eat at a lunch counter rather than permit the owner to control the privilege of who could be served. The Civil Rights Act of 1964 established conclusively the illegality of doing otherwise. More broadly, the groundswell of activist efforts triggered by the sit-in movement augured a new era of direct action. This had concomitant effects on academic governance, faculty rights, and freedom of speech as more people, especially but not exclusively on university campuses, moved to protest. Even as nonviolence inspired some and was condemned by others, it played a decisive role in the early years of the 1960s and shapes efforts for social justice to this day.[3]

But other legacies from the Lawson Affair should leave us feeling uneasier. This episode is a history lesson that, all too easily, lends itself to superficially satisfying conclusions that upon further examination are revealed to be profoundly imperfect. It is no accident that those people involved wrestled internally with all these legal, religious, and social contradictions. As Lawson put it shortly after his expulsion, "the press attack tended to make me a symbol of the movement. But such incidents illustrate an ancient way of escaping an existential moment." To take one example, the active theological work preached and taught by Lawson mapped unevenly upon the wider terrain of white institutionalized religion. Much of the Divinity School faculty's derision toward Nelson derived from scornfulness about the gap between his belated moral clarity and his early fumbled attempts to placate Branscomb. But those academics had their own issues—some self-awareness and advocacy for Lawson, but other agendas too, such as trying to preserve the university's reputation. They felt those conflicting pulls acutely at the time. One Divinity School member was quoted lambasting Branscomb's smugness toward racial change. But he also said explicitly that "I've never really been excited about integration or segregation" and clarified that his "concern" was geared more toward "people than abstractions." Allyship for the civil rights movement took many forms, and produced some positive effects, but often struggled to differentiate between Lawson as a person, a student, and a citizen versus the message of his work. Even those open to nonviolence struggled with the totality of Lawson's convictions and commitment to action. Support for integration rested uncomfortably with direct action.[4]

These musings from the Divinity School faculty indicate just some of the broader ways the civil rights movement triggered widening fractures among the religiously inclined white populace. Many white Christians, particularly those with sentiments aligned with the Social Gospel, responded affirmatively to the theological logic behind civil rights demands. But those from an evangelical or fundamentalist persuasion saw it more pessimistically. For them, the racial change and particularly the specter of race-mixing factored into dismay about law and order issues and the growing involvement of the federal government in dictating social change.[5]

Other "existential moments" devolved into discourse about academic governance and civil disobedience. The consternation about both during the Lawson Affair was real, given that these were and are genuine issues. But focusing on those aspects of the crisis also threatened to sidestep the core racial component of Lawson's expulsion. Irregularities in academic protocols justified the Divinity School stance regardless of Lawson's particulars, to be sure. But Stahlman's and Branscomb's centering of civil disobedience recast the issue in terms of law and order, which gave their personal preferences a supposed veneer of extra authority. These tactics are time-honored ones for white resistance across the eras. And yet, some held out hope that a university should represent something different. One Board of Trust member, Hugh Morgan, voiced support for Lawson throughout the ordeal. His lament about the expulsion was that "we have surrendered truth. We have lowered ourselves to the standards of the merchant and the prejudice of the community." His actual worry was that foundations would not support a university that "surrenders," but the broader point about something lost remains. A university that admits students but does not include them, that is governed almost entirely by the city's power structure and thus perpetuates social imbalances in both places, and that tries to assert civil authority outside of its remit is one that will struggle to live up to the name. For all their struggles and lapses, this is something that the Vanderbilt faculty understood.[6]

And yet, even that noble mentality ignores how the modern university is often designed in such ways. Our gaze upon the events of 1960 from the vantage of today is inevitably influenced by contemporary events as cross-winds of controversy capture college campuses. On quadrangles across the country, political activism, and resultant repression from administrators, has soared as students protest current-day crises or what they perceive as misappropriated values by their university and society at large. More broadly, governmental figures and the wider public attack higher education for indoctrinating wokeness. And beyond those headlines, universities continue to be spaces deeply implicated in problematic ways in power imbalances, whether symbolically, economically, or politically. In that mix, the fraught, ambiguous ideas of freedom of speech and academic freedom continue to be debated anew without any clear resolution. As one historian notes, universities will only continue to fail in their fundamentally contradictory mission of fostering student activity on campus while trying to control its effects.[7]

Echoes of 1960 resonate even today. In March 2024, Vanderbilt students staged a sit-in in Kirkland Hall and invited a reporter to meet with them. That reporter was arrested by Vanderbilt police when he tried to enter the building. The protest stemmed from the university blocking a student petition asking Vanderbilt to divest from financial investments in companies that supported Israel's war efforts against the Palestinian people. At issue was a state law that the Vanderbilt administration cited as potentially interfering with their ability to contract with the State of Tennessee should the divestments take place, an interpretation vigorously contested by the proponents of the petition.[8] The reporter was later released without being charged, although he fervently criticized the university's characterization of what transpired with his detainment.[9] These demonstrations at Vanderbilt, while robust, did not match the intensity or the numbers arrested on other American campuses. But some observers at the time adjudged Vanderbilt's response as particularly harsh, given that Vanderbilt expelled three protestors based on an alleged scuffle with a security guard as the sit-in commenced.[10]

Vanderbilt chancellor Daniel Diermeier rejected those critics of his act who explicitly compared this incident to the Lawson Affair: "I think that is an insult to the . . . heroic work that James Lawson has done," Diermeier said. "Those heroic individuals like Lawson, American heroes, were the ones that suffered the violence or the abuse, and took it without engaging in it themselves. To compare yourself, when you are rushing into a building and injuring a security guard, to the memory of the work that was done by these heroes of the civil rights movement—it's an insult to that, to their memory."[11] The chancellor had already gotten some approbation for his announced policy of "principled neutrality" at Vanderbilt. This was his term for guidelines outlining that the university could best support free speech and healthy academic debate by avoiding taking a position on any matter not directly related to the functioning of the university.[12]

Whatever one thinks about the aptitude of comparing 1960 with 2024, the more recent event highlights much of what makes the ambiguities of the Lawson Affair so searching. The concept of a neutral space for healthy debate and disagreement is a laudatory one—what a university should be. But as institutions, universities are embedded in systems and practices that are anything but neutral, which is precisely why they are both attacked from the outside and vigorously critiqued from within. By deferring to an external law as an absolute authority, whether deserved or not, universities can sidestep this contradiction and avoid further conflict without reputational damage—and indeed, if carefully handled, perhaps even aiding reputational enhancement. One observer writes about how many of these institutions aggressively cracking down on protest today simultaneously promote their own historic student activism as fundamental to their university brand.[13]

Setting aside his handling of the divestment protests, Diermeier's leveraging of historical memory is perhaps even more pertinent. As the civil rights movement changed the conversation about Black freedom in real time during the 1960s, white people constantly readjusted their lenses to reframe some activism as inappropriate, leveraging that judgmentally against what they deemed more palatable. Hence, rejecting both Lawson and Kasper could supposedly acquit one of racial bias. Branscomb used the lack of punishment for white Vanderbilt students who sat-in to justify the notion that Lawson's activism was an outlier worthy of expulsion. The same process canonizes Martin Luther King, despised in his own time but now glorified in contrast to the Black Power movement in public memory and deployed to roll back civil rights progress under the guise of color-blindness.[14] Few protests have been celebrated by wider society in their own historical moment; being permissible would undoubtedly make them much less effective.

In that sense, Nashville's story is the nation's. Far from a parochial case-study, the Lawson Affair exhibits key themes about this era of racial change. Consider how Lawson's activism tried to highlight how segregation worked through both individual sinfulness and complicity with broader structures of inequality. Yet white responses to his expulsion tended to demean either his theology or his constitutional understanding, or both. Or they appreciated his stance but put it parallel or secondary to what white people deemed as more appropriate means or values for obtaining social change. In this way, whether explicitly or unconsciously, white people managed the pace of racial change. And, by managing it, they also sought to control the appropriate messaging about how that change occurred. A particular aspect of Nashville's racial culture is not just the city's tendency to resist progress incessantly before gradually succumbing. But rather it is how Nashville takes so much undue credit for doing the latter that the former is conveniently forgotten. Nonviolent direct action during the Nashville sit-ins exposed the ways selective enforcement of laws fortified racial constructs based on social customs to preserve white supremacy. The attempt to reorient those relationships by the Movement eventually occurred, albeit without the radical Christian intent that Lawson called for and indeed represented. We rightly venerate the sit-ins and those who heeded a higher mission in refusing to bow to an unjust normality. But saluting them for those acts usually comes at the cost of ignoring what they envisioned.

On some level, we should understand and honor James Lawson's choice to forgive Harvie Branscomb, why he did it, and what it meant. That is an act of grace worth emulating. But to forgive the past must not exempt our work in the present and future. The Lawson Affair fundamentally derived from a Black person existing in a white space according to his own personal code while challenging both Black and white people to reconsider their relationship with white supremacy. Whatever rich and illustrative power struggles emerged from that only emphasize how there were, except for James Lawson, no heroes in this story. And why is this so? It is because Lawson's way of being forced each protagonist into a response. Each person confronting Lawson's example had to resolve that challenge to their own institutional loyalties, procedural proprieties, and moral codes. As the crisis compounded, each person found it far too easy to critique the contradictions in other people's stances while ignoring their own. This perhaps explains the central reality that—even while pretending to outsiders that they had prevailed—not a single person was actually satisfied with how the Lawson Affair ended.

More importantly, that reality is underlined by an additional truth: that not a single white person in this book understood Lawson fully on Lawson's own terms or using criteria faithful to Lawson's own perspective. The radical nature of his commitment created serious ruptures in the assured version of segregation that dominated at Vanderbilt, and yet how people responded to Lawson said everything about themselves and much, much less about Lawson himself or his cause. Lawson was correct that unflinching nonviolent direct action could expose the realities of white supremacy in action. His expulsion ultimately showed that this was so, not just in terms of violent reactions to protest, but in more layered ways about institutions and societies constructed on whiteness. Showing how power flexes in different ways—procedurally, rhetorically, ideologically—to stifle change is perhaps the best hope for this story to bear future witness.[15]

Scapegoated by partisan media for telling uncomfortable truths, decried for violating the law yet not permitted due process, scolded for a morality now lionized thanks to historical hindsight—there is the danger that, in rightly elevating Lawson's story, we risk muting what it might mean for Vanderbilt and, by extension, any institution we build or maintain. Yes, we salute Lawson's forgiveness of Branscomb. We see the ways

Vanderbilt honors Lawson today. We understand that apologies matter.

But let us not end the story there, especially given that lingering dissatisfaction of every person involved in this story. That feeling should be ours. What if we returned instead to Lawson's sense of experimentation? What if our universities looked more like his workshops—not even in terms of facilitating activism, but in grappling with new ideas, wrestling with preconceived notions, or listening to other voices to learn how our lives and ideas are shaped and structured? What if we understood Lawson's work as not only fighting segregation but rather building something new, an act less about rebellion and more about creation? As one considers all the "pious certainties," earned and unearned, by the men in this book, perhaps we might also reflect on more ambiguities: how one balances a vision with a method, or a process against objectives, pragmatism with principles, laws and morality, and justice with love. How do we respond when we encounter someone who challenges our conceptions about how to be and act? How do we account for and welcome—on their own terms—people perceived as different who enter traditionally white and elite spaces? How do we nurture commonalities while respecting differences and make exceptions into rules? And indeed . . . how much have we really changed?

There are no easy answers for most of us in times of testing—the mixed, uncertain legacies of the Lawson Affair show that above all else. The best account tracing Cecil Sims's life and career highlights how lawyers "construct worlds" with their work. In his own way, James Lawson tried to build another version of a new world. When those two collided, regardless of how Vanderbilt or white Nashville leveraged their power against him, James Lawson retained his belief in his humanity and his equality. He lived that belief in a rare way: in service of a mix of holistic justice, forceful critiques, and all-encompassing love. His singularity should be the start of the conversation, not the end. He loved despite the flaws, despite the conflicts, despite the ugliness—even when there was precious little to love. He loved because he believed that the benefits of hate were ephemeral. If only some version of that world beckoned for the rest of us.[16]

ACKNOWLEDGMENTS

THIS MONOGRAPH DERIVED FROM a cluster of sources I stumbled upon while writing a different book on modern Nashville's race relations many years ago. That initial volume stands guilty of presenting the same cursory treatment of the Lawson Affair that I mention in this book's introduction. And yet, I could never shake the impulse that this story was a revealing microcosm of broader themes in Southern, civil rights, and higher education history. I am so grateful to all the people who helped make it so.

First and foremost, my immense gratitude goes to Betsy Phillips at Vanderbilt University Press. Her reaction upon hearing about my proposed manuscript was, ahem, shall we say, profanely positive—but, more importantly, hugely heartening. She understood the import of the story and why I wanted to tell it in a particular way. For that, and general and generous counsel, I am deeply appreciative. I also salute her colleagues at VUP who, like her, made the publication process a blessedly smooth one. A special fervent thank you to Deborah May and Laura Scott at the Nashville Public Library for help in accessing sources that helped round out this account.

The process of working through this project was greatly facilitated by select anonymous readers who gave very helpful comments when this manuscript still existed uncomfortably in article format. Two wonderfully supportive but critically engaged reviewers for VUP only heightened that helpfulness. I owe a significant and intricately multifaceted debt to Joe William Trotter: specifically, for the largesse of his Center for Africanamerican Urban Studies and the Economy (CAUSE) which was instrumental many years ago in facilitating work on this project, but more generally for his ongoing mentorship, collaboration, resources, support, and example. And even decades later (!) I still must pay tribute to Timothy S. Huebner for his unwavering support when I was an undergraduate history student (and when it was very much in the balance whether I would repay that investment)!

A special note of fervent thanks for logistical and motivational energy stemming from Randall Stephens, Bruce Baker, George Lewis, Felix Schulz, and Brian Ward, who collectively ensured that I never fully ignored the draft sitting on my hard drive. Brian in particular dug into the weeds with me with a careful reading and splendid feedback—typical of a longer stint of tremendous mentoring and even more enriching friendship. Thanks, fellas.

I suspect my family would lobby for me to acknowledge in print the newest family addition: J. J., Wonder Pup extraordinaire, who got me away from the laptop and out into nature. But finally and forevermore: Michelle, Cameron, and Natalie—my treasures. Thanks for everything that words cannot contain.

NOTES

Introduction

1. The "stillness" portion of this section comes from Mary E. King, *Freedom Song: A Personal Story of the 1960s Civil Rights Movement* (New York: Morrow, 1987), 187–88, but the rest is from Lee C. Camp, "The Architect of the American Civil Rights Movement: James Lawson," *No Small Endeavour* (podcast), March 9, 2023, available at https://www.nosmallendeavor.com/the-architect-of-the-american-civil-rights-movement-james-lawson. See also David Halberstam, *The Children* (New York: Random House, 1998), 31.
2. "Incomparable" in Kelly Miller Smith interview by John Britton, December 22, 1967, Ralph J. Bunche Oral History Collection on the Civil Rights Movement, Moorland-Spingarn Research Center, Howard University. On the civil rights movement in Nashville, see Benjamin Houston, *The Nashville Way: Racial Etiquette and the Struggle for Social Justice in a Southern City* (Athens: University of Georgia Press, 2012); David Halberstam, *The Children*; Linda T. Wynn, "The Dawning of a New Day: The Nashville Sit-Ins, February 13–May 10, 1960," *Tennessee Historical Quarterly* 50, no. 1 (1991): 42–54; Peter Ackerman and Jack Duvall, *A Force More Powerful: A Century of Nonviolent Conflict* (New York: St. Martin's, 2000); Bobby L. Lovett, *The Civil Rights Movement in Tennessee: A Narrative History* (Knoxville: University of Tennessee Press, 2005); Don H. Doyle, *Nashville Since the 1920s* (Knoxville: University of Tennessee Press, 1985); Judith Hoover, "The Nashville Sit-ins: Successful Nonviolent Direct Action Through Rhetorical Invention and Advocacy," in *Like Wildfire: The Rhetoric of the Civil Rights Sit-ins*, ed. Sean Patrick O'Rourke and Lesli K. Pace (Columbia: University of South Carolina Press, 2020), 94–113.
3. On Nashville's importance to SNCC and the civil rights movement see Wesley Hogan, *Many Minds, One Heart: SNCC's Dream for a New America* (Chapel Hill: University of North Carolina, 2007); Gregg L. Michel, *Struggle for a Better South: The Southern Student Organizing Committee, 1964–1969* (New York: Palgrave Macmillan, 2004), 25–26, 91–92; V. P. Franklin, *The Young Crusaders: The Untold Story of the Children*

and Teenagers Who Galvanized the Civil Rights Movement (New York: Beacon Press, 2021), 53, 60; Martin Oppenheimer, *The Sit-In Movement of 1960* (Brooklyn: Carlson, 1989), 126–30; Victoria W. Wolcott, *Living in the Future: Utopianism and the Long Civil Rights Movement* (Chicago: University of Chicago Press, 2022), 174, 177–78; Stephen Haynes, *The Last Segregated Hour: The Memphis Kneel-ins and the Campaign for Southern Church Desegregation* (New York: Oxford University Press, 2012); David P. Cline, *From Reconciliation to Revolution: The Student Interracial Ministry, Liberal Christianity, and the Civil Rights Movement* (Chapel Hill: University of North Carolina Press, 2016), ix–xii, 3–5.

4. Nelson quotation in June 3, 1960, dispatch, box 21, folder 410, Dispatches from *Time* Magazine Correspondents Collection, Houghton Library, Harvard University (hereafter cited as Dispatches from *Time*).
5. Robert McGaw, interviewed by Amy Sturgis, August 2, 1996, Voices of Vanderbilt: An Oral History of Vanderbilt University, https://diglib.library.vanderbilt.edu/voices-processquery.pl?SID=20250704988438490&code=voices&relator=Robert+McGaw&general=&submit=Retrieve+Transcripts; "reviled" in Paul K. Conkin, *Gone with the Ivy: A Biography of Vanderbilt University* (Knoxville: University of Tennessee Press, 1985), 539.
6. "Byzantine" is in Melissa Kean, *Desegregating Private Higher Education in the South: Duke, Emory, Rice, Tulane and Vanderbilt* (Baton Rouge: Louisiana State University Press, 2008), 292n80, with coverage of the Lawson case 196–209; Mark Silk, *Spiritual Politics: Religion and America Since World War II* (New York: Simon and Schuster, 1989), 108–16; Ernest M. Limbo, "James Lawson: The Nashville Civil Rights Movement," in *The Human Tradition in the Civil Rights Movement*, ed. Susan Glisson (Lanham, MD: Rowman & Littlefield, 2006). See also Lovett, *The Civil Rights Movement in Tennessee*, especially 129–31, 141–44 on the Lawson Affair; Hugh Davis Graham, *Crisis In Print: Desegregation and the Press in Tennessee* (Nashville, TN: Vanderbilt University Press, 1967), 200–202; Katherine J. Ballantyne, *Radical Volunteers: Dissent, Desegregation, and Student Power in Tennessee* (Athens: University of Georgia Press, 2024), 41; Jeffrey A. Turner, *Sitting In and Speaking Out: Student Movements in the American South, 1960–1970* (Athens: University of Georgia Press, 2010), 15–42, 84. On Vanderbilt, see Conkin, *Gone with the Ivy* (the Lawson case is the entirety of Chapter 20); Dale A. Johnson, ed., *Vanderbilt Divinity School: Education, Contest and Change* (Nashville, TN: Vanderbilt University Press, 2001), esp. 82–84, 236–46, about its racial legacy. For wider context see Dorothy Dunbar Bromley and Susan McCabe, "Impact of the Sit-in Movement on Academic Freedom," *Negro Educational Review* 12, no. 2 (April 1, 1961), 67–68; Joy Ann Williamson-Lott, *Jim Crow Campus: Higher Education and the Struggle for a New Southern Social Order* (New York: Teachers College Press, 2018), 131; Ibram X. Kendi, *The Black Campus Movement: Black Students and the Racial Reconstitution of Higher Education, 1965–1972* (New York: Springer, 2012); Eddie R. Cole, *The Campus Color Line: College Presidents and the Struggle for Black Freedom* (Princeton, NJ: Princeton University Press, 2020). I have not cited extensively the rich and abundant historiography on religion and civil rights more generally, but see Paul Harvey, *Freedom's Coming: Religious Culture*

and the Shaping of the South from the Civil War Through the Civil Rights Era (Chapel Hill: University of North Carolina Press, 2005), and immediately germane to the Methodist angle is Peter C. Murray, *Methodists and the Crucible of Race, 1930–1975* (Columbia: University of Missouri Press, 2004); Paul William Harris, *A Long Reconstruction: Racial Caste and Reconciliation in the Methodist Episcopal Church* (New York: Oxford University Press, 2022).

7. Warren reference from J. Robert Nelson, September 11, 1976, letter to Woodrow W. Eddins Jr., in Nelson Papers, Vanderbilt University Special Collections (hereafter cited as Nelson Papers). Note: Although correct at the time of research, some of the archival collections cited in this manuscript have been formally processed and/or changed since the research was done.

Chapter 1

1. On Lawson's early life, see the interview with Lawson by David Yellin and Bill Thomas, July 1, 1968, which is originally part of the University of Memphis's Mississippi Valley Collection, but this copy was in box 99, folder 712, Taylor Branch Papers, Wilson Library, University of North Carolina at Chapel Hill (hereafter cited as Branch Papers); chapter 3, "Marching in the Light of Justice: Reflections on the Life of James Lawson" in Byron L. Plumley Jr., "Searching for a Place To Stand: Reflections of Spiritually Rooted Social Activists" (PhD diss., Union Institute, 1993). The point about complementary influences is in Dennis C. Dickerson, "James M. Lawson, Jr.: Methodism, Nonviolence and the Civil Rights Movement," *Methodist History* 52, no. 3 (April 2014): 172; see also Dennis C. Dickerson, "Humanity Defined, Hypocrisy Defied: Sacralizing the Black Freedom Struggle, 1930–60," *Studies in Church History*, no. 60 (2024): 477–510.
2. Anthony Siracusa has placed Lawson's career in a longer lineage of nonviolent civil rights theoreticians, coining the term "the politics of being" for Lawson's contribution to that intellectual legacy: see Anthony Siracusa, *Nonviolence Before King: The Politics of Being and the Black Freedom Struggle* (Chapel Hill: University of North Carolina Press, 2021). Quotation from Anthony C. Siracusa, "Developing an American *Ahimsa*: The Reverend James M. Lawson Jr.'s Paradigm of Protest" (BA thesis, Rhodes College, 2009), 9–10, 16; Lawson interview, box 99, folder 712, Branch Papers; on Methodist networks, see interview with James Lawson (F-0029) by Dallas A. Blanchard, October 24, 1983, pgs. 27–28, in Southern Oral History Program Collection, UNC (hereafter cited as SOHP); Scott Patterson McDuffie, "James Lawson: Leading Architect and Educator of Nonviolence and Nonviolent Direct Action Protest Strategies During the Student Sit-in Movement of 1960" (MA thesis, North Carolina State University, 2007); "marked man" was the phrasing of Divinity School professor James Glasse, quoted in *Jet* magazine, June 16, 1960.
3. Halberstam, *The Children*, 11–24; Lawson interview, box 99, folder 712, Branch Papers; Johnson et al., "The Lawson Affair"; Aldon D. Morris, *The Origins of the Civil Rights Movement* (New York: Simon and Schuster, 1984), 157, 162–64.

4. The fullest and latest account of this process is Anthony C. Siracusa, "From Pacifism to Resistance: The Evolution of Nonviolence in Wartime America," *Journal of Civil and Human Rights* 3, no. 1 (Spring/Summer 2017), 57–77, and Siracusa, *Nonviolence Before King*. See also Joseph Kip Kosek, "Religion and Nonviolence in American History," *Religion Compass*, no. 6 (2012), 402–13; Sudarshan Kapur, *Raising Up a Prophet: The African-American Encounter with Gandhi* (Boston: Beacon Press, 1992); Nico Slate, *Colored Cosmopolitanism: The Shared Struggle for Freedom in the United States and India* (Cambridge, MA: Harvard University Press, 2012).
5. A quintessential example of this stress on Nashville's racial possibility is in the interview with Everett Tilson by Benjamin Houston, August 30, 2005, Samuel Proctor Oral History Program, University of Florida (hereafter cited as Proctor Oral History).
6. Katrina Marie Sanders-Cassell, *Intelligent and Effective Direction: The Fisk University Race Relations Institute and the Struggle for Civil Rights, 1944–1969* (New York: Peter Lang, 2005); Richard Robbins, *Sidelines Activist: Charles S. Johnson and the Struggle for Civil Rights* (Jackson: University Press of Mississippi, 1996); Will Sarvis. "Leaders in the Court and Community: Z. Alexander Looby, Avon N. Williams, Jr., and the Legal Fight for Civil Rights in Tennessee, 1940–1970," *Journal of African American History* 88, no. 1 (2003): 42–58; Keith W. Berry, "Charles S. Johnson, Fisk University, and the Struggle for Civil Rights, 1945–1970" (PhD dissertation, Florida State University, 2005).
7. Merrill M. Hawkins, *Will Campbell: Radical Prophet of the South* (Macon, GA: Mercer University Press, 1997); Charles W. Eagles, "The Closing of Mississippi Society: Will Campbell, 'The $64,000 Question,' and Religious Emphasis Week at the University of Mississippi," *Journal of Southern History* 67, no. 2 (2001): 331–72; Benjamin Houston, "'The Aquinas of the Rednecks': Reconciliation, the Southern Character, and the Bootleg Ministry of Will D. Campbell," *The Sixties* 4, no. 2 (2011): 135–50. On the other groups, see Houston, *The Nashville Way*, 39–42; Tilson interview by Houston, Proctor Oral History, 8–12.
8. Halberstam, *The Children*, 111. See Houston, *The Nashville Way*, 2–7, 28–36. John Seigenthaler, Nashville newspaper editor, said explicitly that he saw power in Nashville in terms of "three interlocking directorates . . . the Chamber of Commerce, the Vanderbilt University Board of Trust, and the Belle Meade Country Club" in interview with Benjamin Houston, June 16, 2003, pg. 3, Proctor Oral History. For a sense of white Nashville's attitudes, see the self-mythology represented in the *New York Post*, March 30, 1960 (copy in box 55, folder "Sit-Downs in South," James Lawson Jr. Papers, Vanderbilt University Special Collections [hereafter cited as Lawson Papers]), and John Compton, interview with Benjamin Houston, June 11, 2003, in Proctor Oral History, 7.
9. Glenda Elizabeth Gilmore treats the careers of Alexander, Kester, and West in *Defying Dixie: The Radical Roots of Civil Rights, 1919–1950* (New York: W.W. Norton, 2008). See also Doyle, *Nashville Since the 1920s*, 177; John Egerton, *Speak Now Against the Day: The Generation Before the Civil Rights Movement in the South* (Chapel Hill: University of North Carolina Press, 1995), especially 77–79; on Weatherford, 44, 47; on Alexander, 122–23; on The Fugitives and Agrarians, 61–70; on Kester, 124–26,

154; on West, 158–59; on Taylor, 77–79, 289–92. See also the Don West interview, by Jacquelyn Hall and Ray Faherty (E-0016), January 22, 1975, SOHP. See also Morton Sosna, *In Search of the Silent South: Southern Liberals and the Race Issue* (New York: Columbia University Press, 1977).

10. On the Agrarians, see John T. Kneebone, *Southern Liberal Journalists and the Issue of Race, 1920–1944* (Chapel Hill: University of North Carolina Press, 1985), especially chapter 4 on the Agrarians, and Paul K. Conkin, *The Southern Agrarians* (Knoxville: University of Tennessee Press, 1988); Emily Bingham and Thomas A. Underwood, eds., *The Southern Agrarians and the New Deal: Essays After I'll Take My Stand* (Charlottesville: University of Virginia Press, 2001); Paul V. Murphy, *The Rebuke of History: The Southern Agrarians and American Conservative Thought* (Chapel Hill: University of North Carolina Press, 2003).
11. On Davidson and the TFCG, see Betsy Phillips, *Dynamite Nashville: Unmasking the FBI, KKK, and the Bombers Beyond Their Control* (Nashville, TN: Third Man Books, 2024); Benjamin Houston, "Donald Davidson and the Segregationist Intellect," in *Southern Character: Essays in Honor of Bertram Wyatt-Brown*, ed. Lisa Tendrich Frank and Daniel Kilbride (Gainesville: University Press of Florida, 2011), 160–77; Paul V. Murphy, "The Social Memory of the South: Donald Davidson and the Tennessee Past," *Tennessee Historical Quarterly* 55, no. 3 (Fall 1996): 257–69; Mark Royden Winchell, *Where No Flag Flies: Donald Davidson and the Southern Resistance* (Columbia: University of Missouri Press, 2000).
12. On Vanderbilt's repressiveness, see Egerton, *Speak Now*, 129, 236, 431–32, 446. On Davidson not being disciplined, see the *Tennessean*, March 4, 1960.
13. Kean, *Desegregating Private Higher Education*, 6; Peter Wallenstein, ed., *Higher Education and the Civil Rights Movement: White Supremacy, Black Southerners, and College Campuses* (Gainesville: University Press of Florida, 2008); Joy Ann Williamson-Lott, "The Battle over Power, Control, and Academic Freedom at Southern Institutions of Higher Education, 1955–1965," *Journal of Southern History* 79, no. 4 (November 2013), 879–920; Harold S. Wechsler and Steven J. Diner, *Unwelcome Guests: A History of Access to American Higher Education* (Baltimore, MD: Johns Hopkins University Press, 2021). See Conkin, *Gone with the Ivy*, 457, on Vanderbilt's financial needs.
14. Conkin, *Gone with the Ivy*, 453, 546–47. See the Executive Committee listing in the *Tennessean*, March 3, 1960. For an interesting comparison about reactions from other campuses to university integration, see chapter 2 in Robert Cohen, *Confronting Jim Crow: Race, Memory, and the University of Georgia in the Twentieth Century* (Chapel Hill: University of North Carolina Press, 2024).
15. Quotations in Lovett, *Civil Rights Movement*, 129, and Bill Carey, *Chancellors, Commodores and Coeds: A History of Vanderbilt University* (Nashville, TN: Clearbook Press, 2003) 260. On Stahlman, see Houston, *The Nashville Way*, 39; Halberstam, *The Children*, throughout but in terms of Vanderbilt, 116, 121, 189, 190, 198, 201, 202.
16. Kean, *Desegregating Higher Education*, 8. On Sims, see Daniel J. Sharfstein, "Brown, Massive Resistance, and the Lawyer's View: A Nashville Story," *Vanderbilt Law Review* 74, no. 5 (October 2021): 1,435–66.
17. Conkin, *Gone with the Ivy*, 453–55, 460.

18. On Branscomb, see Conkin, *Gone with the Ivy*, 449–53, 502–3, and Kean, *Desegregating Higher Education*, 12–17; on Branscomb's handling of race at Duke, see Melissa Kean, "The Early, Unsuccessful Effort to Desegregate Duke University," *Journal of Blacks in Higher Education*, no. 62 (2008): 84–86. An account of the early steps of Vanderbilt desegregation is in Robert McGaw, "A Policy that the University Can Defend," *Vanderbilt Alumnus* (November–December 1956), 12–15.
19. On the diner incident, see Halberstam, *The Children*, 193; Conkin, *Gone with the Ivy*, 431–32, 449–53, and, on Branscomb's racial views, 540–46. See also Conkin on other controversies weathered by Branscomb, including on 502–3 regarding theologian Nels Ferre.
20. The departmental name was changed from the School of Religion to the Divinity School in 1956. Williamson-Lott, "The Battle over Power," 882; James P. Byrd Jr., "Charting a New Vision: The School of Religion" in Johnson, *Vanderbilt Divinity School*, 82.
21. Melissa Kean has the finest account of Branscomb negotiating this process, see *Desegregating Higher Education*, 68–76. See also Peter J. Paris, "The African American Presence in the Divinity School" in Johnson, *Vanderbilt Divinity School*, 236–39; Katherine J. Ballantyne, *Radical Volunteers*, 23–25, 28–29, 31. There are materials pertaining to later desegregation comparators from other universities in box 7, folder 2, Harold S. Vanderbilt Papers, VUSC. On Sewanee, see Gardiner H. Shattuck Jr., *Episcopalians and Race: Civil War to Civil Rights* (Lexington: University Press of Kentucky, 2014); and "'The Real Issue': A Reconsideration of the Turbulent Desegregation of Sewanee's School of Theology, 1952–1953, Part I," *Meridiana* (blog), Roberson Project on Slavery, Race and Reconciliation, December 11, 2018, https://meridiana.sewanee.edu/2018/12/11/the-real-issue-a-reconsideration-of-the-turbulent-desegregation-of-sewanees-school-of-theology-1952-1953-part-i.
22. On the Divinity School and Nelson, see Paul Conkin, *Gone with the Ivy*, 501–2.
23. Paris, "The African American Presence in the Divinity School," 236–39. See also the website of the Bishop Joseph Johnson History Project, https://bishopjosephjohnson.org/ and "Bishop Joseph Johnson," Bishop Joseph Johnson Black Cultural Center, Vanderbilt University, https://www.vanderbilt.edu/bcc/bishop-joseph-johnson. Halberstam, *The Children*, 8, maintains that there was a gentleman's agreement with the school's dean that Black students would "be invisible men, not seen and not heard, if at all possible, outside of the classroom."
24. Daniel J. Sharfstein, "Brown, Massive Resistance," 1,455; on the law school desegregation process, see Kean, *Desegregating Higher Education*, 99–104.
25. Johnson et al., "The Lawson Affair," 136–37; Nelson, "Strictly Confidential," pgs. 1, 3, Nelson Papers; Kean, *Desegregating Higher Education*, 12–17; on Lawson's disregard of racial boundaries, see Wallace Westfeldt, *New York Herald Tribune*, June 6, 1960; Halberstam, *The Children*, 122, 124–25. Lawson discussed his impressions of his faculty members in Blanchard interview, SOHP.
26. C. T. Vivian and Steve Fiffer, *It's in the Action: Memories of a Nonviolent Warrior* (Montgomery, AL: NewSouth Books, 2021), 37; see also Halberstam, *The Children*, 57;

and Cynthia Griggs Fleming, "C. T. Vivian: Disciple of Assertive Nonviolence," *AME Church Review* 118, no. 387 (July–September 2002): 26–54.

27. How the school integration crisis exposed Nashville's mythology of good race relations was the core argument of Roger L. Shinn, "Symbolic Roles in Little Rock and Nashville," *Christianity and Crisis*, February 3, 1958, 5. See also Houston, *The Nashville Way*, 74–81; Sharfstein, "*Brown*, Massive Resistance," 1,455–61; Kean, *Desegregating*, 98.
28. Houston, *The Nashville Way*, 82–86.
29. Quotations in Dickerson, "James M. Lawson, Jr.," 168, 170. See also Larry W. Isaac et al., "'Movement Schools' and Dialogical Diffusion of Nonviolent Praxis: Nashville Workshops in the Southern Civil Rights Movement," in *Nonviolent Conflict and Civil Resistance*, ed. Sharon Erickson Nepstead and Lester R. Kurtz (Leeds, UK: Emerald Publishing, 2012).
30. Hogan, *Many Minds, One Heart*, chapter 1; Anthony C. Siracusa, "'The Doctrine of Truth's Many Sides': Jain Religion, James Lawson, and the Politics of Nonviolence in the Black Freedom Struggle," *West Tennessee Historical Society Papers*, no. 70 (2016), 21–36.
31. Block quotation in James Lawson interview, conducted by Blackside Inc. on December 2, 1985, for "Eyes on the Prize: America's Civil Rights Years (1954–1965)," Eyes on the Prize Interviews, Film and Media Archive, Henry Hampton Collection, Washington University Libraries; Lawson in box 99, folder 712, Branch Papers; Nico Slate, "The Drama of Nonviolence: Theatre as Education within the American Civil Rights Movement," *Research in Drama Education* 27, no. 1 (2022), 11.
32. Lawson, Eyes on the Prize interview.
33. Peter A. Kuryla, "James Lawson, Jr., and the 1968 Memphis Sanitation Workers' Strike," *AME Church Review* (July–September 2002), 57; Anthony C. Siracusa, "Understanding Militant Non-violence within Memphis' Modern Civil Rights Movement: The Leadership and Witness of the Rev. James M. Lawson Jr." (Memphis: Rhodes College Institute for Regional Studies, 2007), 4.
34. Lawson, Eyes on the Prize interview; Lawson in May 26, 1960, statement, pgs. 1–2, box 29, folder "Chancellor's Files – Lawson," Centennial History Project Papers, VUSC (hereafter cited as Centennial History Project).
35. Wesley Hogan, *Many Minds, One Heart*, 19, 20, 26; Johnson et al., "The Lawson Affair," 140. On the sit-in movement coming to Nashville, see Taylor Branch, *Parting the Waters: America in the King Years, 1965–1963* (New York: Simon & Schuster, 2007), 272–75.
36. James M. Lawson Jr., interview with Robert Penn Warren, March 17, 1964, tape 1, transcript pg. 3, available at "Robert Penn Warren's *Who Speaks for the Negro?*: An Archival Collection," https://whospeaks.library.vanderbilt.edu/interview/james-m-lawson-jr (hereafter cited as Lawson interview with Warren); Halberstam, *The Children*, 113; on West, see David Halberstam, "A Good City Gone Ugly," *The Reporter*, March 31, 1960, 19; "heroically unavailable" quotation in June 3, 1960, box 21, folder 410, Dispatches from *Time*.

37. Interview with James Lawson conducted by Joan Beifuss and Bill Thomas, July 21, 1969, interview 247, series vi, mss 178, The Search for Meaning Committee Papers, Special Collections Department, University of Memphis Libraries (hereafter cited as Search for Meaning Committee Papers); Everett Tilson, "The Ugly Rebel" (unpublished mss., copy in possession of the author), 9–10.
38. Again, the notion of Lawson's nonviolent "experiment" is echoed by the emphasis on role-play and improvisation in nonviolence, see Slate, "The Drama of Nonviolence," 11. See also Susan Leigh Foster, "Choreographies of Protest," *Theatre Journal* 55, no. 3 (2003): 395–412; Houston, *The Nashville Way*, chapter 3.
39. Lawson interview with Warren, tape 1, transcript pg. 3–4. The detail about the judge is in Paul Bushnell and Pam Muirhead, "Paul Bushnell: Nashville Memories," Oral Histories, Indiana Wesleyan University Digital Commons, March 14, 2003, 2, https://digitalcommons.iwu.edu/oral_hist/50.
40. Lawson interview, Search for Meaning Committee Papers; Halberstam, "A Good City Gone Ugly," 18. On police repression in Nashville, see Gregg L. Michel, *Spying on Students: The FBI, Red Squads, and Student Activists in the 1960s South* (Baton Rouge: Louisiana State University Press, 2024) and Houston, *The Nashville Way*, 165–66.

Chapter 2

1. J. Robert Nelson, "Strictly Confidential: The Case of James M. Lawson," March 6, 1960, folder "Original and Essential Letters of the Vanderbilt Divinity School Crisis, Spring 1960" (hereafter "Original and Essential Letters"), Nelson Papers.
2. Lawson interview, Search for Meaning Committee Papers; Arthur L. Foster, Chronology of Events, box 29, folder "Divinity School Students – Lawson," 4–5, Centennial History Project Papers, VUSC (hereafter cited as Foster Chronology).
3. Christopher W. Schmidt, *The Sit-Ins: Protest and Legal Change in the Civil Rights Era* (Chicago: University of Chicago Press, 2018), 7. I added italics for clarity.
4. George Lewis, *Massive Resistance: The White Response to the Civil Rights Movement* (London: Bloomsbury Academic, 2006), 132–35.
5. Schmidt, *The Sit-Ins*, 9; Lawson in Foster Chronology, 5; Sims's reactions to the sit-ins and races eating together in Sharfstein, "Brown, Massive Resistance," 1,462–64.
6. See the Chattanooga newspaper coverage about this legal dilemma: *News-Free Press*, May 11, 1960, l; and also Wallace Westfeldt, "A Report on Nashville," 2–4, copy in box 111, folder 126, Lawson Papers. For the segregationist take on this, see the March 18, 1960, letter to Madison Sarratt from TCFG member L. V. DuBose, in box 2, folder "Lawson Case" (2 of 2), Madison Sarratt Papers, VUSC. Rather ironically given Lawson's meeting with West, DuBose called the language of those sitting in a "gimmick" of rhetoric covering the nefarious intentions of "professional do-gooders."
7. The fullest rendition of Lawson's rejoinder to West is actually in Everett Tilson, "The Ugly Rebel," 27–29, although recounted secondhand; see also the Lawson interview, Search for Meaning Committee Papers; and Lawson's May 26, 1960, account, box 29,

folder "Chancellor's Files - Lawson," Centennial History Project. See also Everett Tilson in *The Christian Century*, April 27, 1960, where he refers to three people present who understood the gimmick line as referring specifically to Hosse's use of local ordinances to justify the arrests.

8. On Lawson's "gimmick" quotation see Houston, *The Nashville Way*, 102–3; Halberstam, "A Good City Gone Ugly," 17–19. Lawson's later clarification is in his pgs. 3–4, May 26, 1960, statement, box 29, folder "Chancellor's Files - Lawson," Centennial History Project. Lawson discusses his nonviolent approach, including the need to suffer the legal consequences, in the Lawson interview with Warren, tape 1, transcript pg. 6.
9. Foster Chronology, 4–5.
10. See the *Tennessean*, March 1, 1960; Galatians detail in *Christian Century*, March 23, 1960, 342; David E. Sumner, "The Publisher and the Preacher: Racial Conflict at Vanderbilt University," *Tennessee Historical Quarterly* 56, no. 1 (1997), 36, 38; Johnson et al., "The Lawson Affair," 144; Foster Chronology, 5, 7. Both Lawson and Will D. Campbell criticized the *Tennessean*'s coverage specifically; Stahlman's role with the *Banner* should not obscure this broader point about media coverage here.
11. *Chattanooga Times*, March 1, 1960. On Chattanooga reports, see "Strictly Confidential," pgs. 1, 3, and insert, Nelson Papers. The differing media coverage of this meeting is covered in David Sumner, "The Local Press and the Nashville Student Movement, 1960" (PhD diss., University of Tennessee, 1989), 37–38, 75–81, 172–74; Johnson et al., "The Lawson Affair," 145–46. Student quotation in *Tennessean*, March 9, 1960.
12. On West and Branscomb, see Tilson, "The Ugly Rebel," 10; on West's anxiety (West was "scared for the effect of his actions on his political future"), see the May 16, 1960, letter from Charles Roos to Branscomb, "Chancellor's files 1–44," box 29, folder "Kirkland Divinity School Students Lawson," Centennial History Project. On Branscomb and Nelson, see "Strictly Confidential," Nelson Papers.
13. "Strictly Confidential," Nelson Papers, 3; Halberstam, *The Children*, 202.
14. "Strictly Confidential," pgs. 1, 3, Nelson Papers; Kean, *Desegregating Higher Education*, 73; Conkin, *Gone with the Ivy*, 551. On the "panty raid" context, see Jonathan Day, "A Breech in the Wall: The Vanderbilt University Student Community and the 1960s" (BA thesis, Vanderbilt University, 1996), 11–12.
15. "Evasive" in "Strictly Confidential," pg. 2, see also 3–4, Nelson Papers.
16. Lawson's response in appendix 1 of the report in box 29, "Chancellor's Files 1–44," folder "Lawson," Centennial History Project; "Strictly Confidential," pgs. 3–4, Nelson Papers. At this point, Lawson also had an interview with Harrison Salisbury in *The New York Times* and a press conference with Nashville media, none of which helped his case. Salisbury quoted him as speaking "with bitterness" about the legal tricks used to thwart racial progress—see *New York Times*, March 2, 1960.
17. Lawson in box 29 "Chancellor's Files 1–44," folder "Lawson," Centennial History Project; Lawson interview with Warren, tape 1, transcript pg. 11.
18. Second statement, May 26, 1960, in appendix ii, pgs. 7–8, box 29, "Chancellor's Files 1–44," folder "Lawson," Centennial History Project; "Strictly Confidential," pgs. 3–4, Nelson Papers.

19. Typescript, May 26, 1960, pg. 10, in box 29 "Chancellor's Files 1–44," folder "Lawson," Centennial History Project; "Strictly Confidential," pg. 4, Nelson Papers. See also McGaw's account of the meeting in the retroactive memo to Branscomb marked "rec'd 10/26/60" in box 29, folder "Chancellor's Files, Kirkland Hall re: Lawson," Centennial History Papers. Lawson's statement reprinted in full in *Tennessean*, March 3, 1960.
20. "Strictly Confidential," pgs. 4–5, Nelson Papers; "gratuitous insult" quotation and Lawson's admission record information in Branscomb, "The Lawson Episode: The Role of Dean Robert Nelson," pg. 3, box 29, folder "Harvie Branscomb on James Lawson," Centennial History Project; "Addendum to the Chancellor's Report to the Board of Trust of Vanderbilt University," October 7, 1960, in folder 14, box V-29, page d, Stahlman Papers, VUSC (hereafter cited as Stahlman Papers); *Nashville Banner*, March 3, 1960.
21. "Strictly Confidential," Nelson Papers. The point about Stahlman and draft-dodging is in Halberstam, *The Children*, 189.
22. "Strictly Confidential," Nelson Papers.
23. "Strictly Confidential," pgs. 2, 6, Nelson Papers. Nelson claimed later that Branscomb was petrified of racial incidents "lest the presidents of Duke and Tulane have the laugh on him for integrating"; the irony was that nine months later both those schools desegregated. See April 22, 1961, letter to "Jim," folder "Original and Essential Letters," Nelson Papers. There was also a bizarre point of confusion in the committee's conversation over how to interpret Lawson's arrest record that Nelson blamed on Sims, but Branscomb blamed on Nelson—one example among far too many to recount as to how the smallest of details were being interpreted in the worst possible light.
24. Note some divergences here: Branscomb accused Nelson of being unwilling to give a recommendation to the board (Branscomb, "The Lawson Episode: The Role of Dean Robert Nelson," pg. 3, in box 29, folder "Harvie Branscomb on James Lawson," Centennial History Project), whereas Nelson claims he initially asked them to postpone any decision and only subsequently, based on ensuing discussions, volunteered to broker the withdrawal arrangement. See also "Address to the Princeton University Chapter of the AAUP, April 11, 1961," pg. 1, folder "Letters from Princeton," Nelson Papers. This account stresses the issues from the perspective of academic freedom given who Nelson was addressing.
25. "Strictly Confidential," pgs. 6–8, Nelson Papers.
26. Halberstam, *The Children*, 202–5; "Strictly Confidential," pgs. 6–8, Nelson Papers. Quotations from Campbell in Tom Royals, ed., *Conversations with Will D. Campbell* (Jackson: University Press of Mississippi, 2018), 52–53.
27. "Strictly Confidential," pgs. 6–8, Nelson Papers. On Harold S. Vanderbilt, see Conkin, *Gone with the Ivy*, 454–55.
28. Nelson observation in his letter to Tilson, November 7, 1960, folder "Correspondence from Princeton," Nelson Papers.
29. Johnson et al., "The Lawson Affair," 141–42; Branscomb statement in *Tennessean*, March 4, 1960; Houston, *The Nashville Way*, 106; Halberstam, *The Children*, 206–7; Lovett, *The Civil Rights Movement*, 130; Lawson interview with Warren, tape 1,

transcript pg. 13; Tilson, "Ugly Rebel," 30; and Foster Chronology, 13–14; Bushnell and Muirhead, "Paul Bushnell."

30. See the *Nashville Banner*, March 3, 1960; March 4, 1960 (editorial); June 7, 1960 (reprinting *Louisville Courier-Journal*, June 3, 1960, editorial); June 8, 1960 (reprinting June 3 *Memphis Commercial-Appeal* editorial); Foster Chronology, 12–13; *New York Times*, March 4, 1960. A range of newspaper coverage is contained in box 7 of the Harvie Branscomb Papers, VUSC. Foster Chronology, 9, notes how Branscomb and Stahlman used the same logic and rationale in much of their writings on the matter. See also the "James Lawson" file, *Nashville Banner* clippings collection, Nashville Room, Nashville Public Library (hereafter cited as Nashville Room). On Stahlman's enmity to Lawson, see David Sumner, "The Publisher and the Preacher: Racial Conflict at Vanderbilt University," *Tennessee Historical Quarterly*, 56, no. 1 (1997), 36, 38; Kean, *Desegregating Higher Education*, 197; Tilson, "Ugly Rebel," 63–66; on rumor-mongering and death threats, see A. W. Martin Jr., "The Lawson Affair, the Sit-Ins, and Beyond," *Tennessee Historical Quarterly* 75, no. 2 (Summer 2016), 142–65.
31. NCLC response to Branscomb in *Christian Century*, April 20, 1960 (copy in Branscomb, box 29 "Chancellor's files 1–44," folder "Kirkland Divinity School Students Lawson," Centennial History Project); *Nashville Globe*, March 18, 1960; "Barabbas" in *Nashville News Star*, June 12, 1960. The *Globe* shut down shortly after this issue and only a few issues of the *News Star* were published, so there is scant coverage of the Lawson case among local Black newspapers. There is one *News Star* editorial, June 12, 1960, that I was unable to find anywhere else reproduced in Tilson, "Ugly Rebel," 36–37. Lawson's legal reading was upheld in *Garner v. Louisiana*, 368 U.S. (1961)—see John Kirk, "Another Side of the Sit-Ins: Nonviolent Direct Action, the Courts, and the Constitution," in *From Sit-Ins to SNCC: The Student Civil Rights Movements in the 1960s*, ed. Iwan Morgan and Philip Davies (Gainesville: University Press of Florida, 2012), 31.
32. Foster Chronology, 14. Lawson believed in a policy of not paying bail money and embracing jail, on the logic that the latter increased the moral weight of the protestor and removed the stigma of prison, and the former because bail money only went to the judicial structures that were perpetuating injustice. Everett Tilson had to convince C. T. Vivian and Diane Nash to allow Lawson to accept the money, arguing that it was symbolic that such a large amount was raised wholly by the white community on behalf of the sit-ins. In retrospect, Tilson allowed that Vivian's resistance to this argument may have been right. He also stressed that it was he and Foster who were the conduits for bailing Lawson out, which is often either attributed to Nelson or generically to the Divinity School faculty. Tilson interview, pgs. 37–38, Proctor Oral History.
33. The eleven signees acted in part because Cecil Sims had advised that the new charge against Lawson on state charges of conspiracy to restrain trade was serious and the failure to provide bail would hurt Lawson's chances ("Strictly Confidential," pg. 8, Nelson Papers). On the petition and its signees, see *Tennessean*, March 9, 1960; details on the counter-petition in Conkin, *Gone with the Ivy*, 555. See also *New York Times*, March 4, 1960; *Tennessean*, March 4, 1960.

34. *Time*, June 13, 1960, 59–60; *Washington Post* (editorial), June 1, 1960, Everett Tilson File, Nashville Room; Foster Chronology, 45–46, 52. Kean, *Desegregating Higher Education*, 294n98, describes Branscomb's use of news leaks to control public understanding.
35. Quotations in *Christian Century*, March 23, 1960, 342; Tilson letter, March 30, 1960 (copy in possession of the author). See also the coverage in *Christian Century*, March 16, 1960, 309; March 30, 1960, 379; April 6, 1960, 405; April 27, 1960, 514–15; June 8, 1960, 685–86; June 29, 1960, 764. See especially the exchange between *The Christian Century* and Branscomb, April 13, 1960, 436, 444, recapped in the *Tennessean*, April 12, 1960. For background on the periodical, see Elesha J. Coffman, *The Christian Century and the Rise of the Protestant Mainline* (New York: Oxford University Press, 2013). Nelson was an editor at large with *Christian Century*. Branscomb asked Nelson to co-sign on his correspondence, but Nelson supported the periodical's stance instead (Nelson letter to James Adams, November 6, 1960, pg. 3, folder "Letters from Princeton," Nelson Papers). Adams was one of the investigators from the American Association of Theological Schools who censured the university after the Lawson Affair. Arthur Foster also had discussions with the editor of the *Christian Advocate* that were deployed editorially; see Foster Chronology, 100. Tilson had some critical words of a "friend" in the Divinity School, unnamed but presumably Nelson by context, although the two worked in tandem: March 31, 1960, letter to Theodore Gill (copy in possession of the author). For more on Tilson, see Paul Burnam, "Everett Tilson: Pioneer in the Condemnation of White Privilege," *Ohio History* 127, no. 1 (Spring 2020), 87–103.
36. Foster Chronology, 5, 7–8; Nelson in *Christian Century*, August 10, 1960, 921–925; "Strictly Confidential," pg. 4, Nelson Papers; memo to University Senate, March 11, 1960, and memo to Bard Thompson from Sellers and Silberman, April 5, 1960, both in folder "Original and Essential Letters," Nelson Papers.
37. Foster Chronology, 10–12; Tilson, "Ugly Rebel," 11; Nelson, *Christian Century*, August 10, 1960, 922. The Gandhi crack is in Nelson, Princeton AAUP document, 1, Nelson Papers.
38. Presentation to University Senate, March 11, 1960, in folder "Original and Essential Letters," Nelson Papers; "Sandbagged" in Roos interview by Kathy Bennett, May 19, 2004, Civil Rights Oral History Project Collection, Civil Rights Room, Special Collections Division, Nashville Public Library (hereafter cited as Oral History Project, NPL). See minutes of March 15 meeting in box 4, folder "Correspondence—Vanderbilt University—James Lawson Case and Student Disciplinary Procedure, 1960," Edmund M. Morgan Jr. Papers, VUSC.
39. Foster Chronology, 5, 8; memo to University Senate, March 11, 1960; memo to Bard Thompson from Sellers and Silberman, April 5, 1960. Lawson describes his conscious decision to minimize the role of Vanderbilt students and faculty in sit-in activities in his SOHP interview, pgs. 6, 13–15. On the criticism from visiting speakers, see Foster Chronology, 18–19; *Tennessean*, March 22 and 23, 1960. See also Tilson interview, pgs. 32–34, Proctor Oral History. See Nelson's letters gauging the possibility of Lawson enrolling at these schools in box 21, folder 20, Lawson Papers.

40. Branscomb to Roos, May 16, 1960, and Roos to Branscomb, May 19, 1960, in Branscomb, box 29 "Chancellor's files 1–44," folder "Kirkland Divinity School Students Lawson," Centennial History Project; Roos's later reflections are in Johnson et al., "The Lawson Affair," 143–45; on medical school, see *Tennessean*, May 6, 1960.
41. Foster Chronology, 20–25.
42. On the consultations, see Silberman, report at AAUP meeting, June 8, 1960, folder "Original and Essential Letters," Nelson Papers; Foster Chronology, 20–23; Branscomb's statement in *Tennessean*, March 30, 1960.
43. Journalist quotation in March 15, 1960, filing, box 20, folder 399, Dispatches from *Time*.
44. Consider the similar reading of the situation, alongside the scapegoating and divide-and-conquer strategies, as seen by James M. Wolfe in the letter to Nelson, July 13, 1960, "Letters in re: resignation," Nelson Papers.
45. Foster Chronology, 25–28. On the Beach Committee, see Conkin, *Gone with the Ivy*, 555; *Nashville Banner*, June 3, 1960; Nelson letter to James Adams, November 6, 1960, pgs. 4–5, folder "Letters from Princeton," Nelson Papers; the materials in box 4, folder "Correspondence—Vanderbilt University—James Lawson Case and Student Disciplinary Procedure, 1960," Morgan Papers, VUSC.
46. Nelson in August 10, 1960, *Christian Century*, 923. See also Branscomb's March 8, 1960, address to the Arts and Science Faculty, in box 20, folder "Lawson Case—Press Releases and Memoranda," Hyatt Papers, VUSC.
47. Nelson, *Christian Century*, August 10, 1960, 923; Nelson letter to James Adams, November 6, 1960, pg. 4, folder "Letters from Princeton," Nelson Papers.
48. On the luncheon, see Nelson letter to James Adams, November 6, 1960, pg. 3, folder "Letters from Princeton," Nelson Papers; Foster Chronology, 34.
49. Foster Chronology, 17; Johnson et al., "The Lawson Affair," 147.
50. Letter to Nelson from James Sellers, May 25, 1960, Nelson Papers; Nelson letter to James Adams, November 6, 1960, pgs. 4–5, folder "Letters from Princeton," Nelson Papers; Tilson interview with Houston, Proctor Oral History, 33–34.
51. Foster Chronology, 27–32.
52. On the May 10 events, see Houston, *The Nashville Way*, 118–22. On Lawson's reapplication, see Foster Chronology, 29–30; Johnson et al., "The Lawson Affair," 148–49, 157–58. See Tilson, "Ugly Rebel," 32–33, regarding the Beach Committee report. Divinity School member Philip Hyatt also kept a short chronology of May events; he was the chief dissenter to the other Divinity School members. He commented on his perspective that his colleagues were "playing politics" and also on his candid conversations with Nelson—see May 14 chronology in box 20, folder "Lawson Case—Press Releases and Memoranda," in Hyatt Papers, VUSC.
53. This meeting is treated in detail by Nelson letter to James Adams, November 6, 1960, folder "Letters from Princeton," pg. 5, Nelson Papers. See also "comment to faculty," May 24, 1960, for Nelson's quotations; letter to Nelson from James Sellers, May 25, 1960, for Sellers defending himself against allegations from other faculty members; and "talk with Paul Sanders," November 26, 1960, all in folder "Original and Essential Letters," Nelson Papers. Also see Foster Chronology, 28–34.

54. Foster Chronology, 29, 34–36, 42; Nelson letter to James Adams, November 6, 1960, pgs. 5–6, folder "Letters from Princeton," Nelson Papers; "Notes on Conversation with Chancellor Branscomb, May 26, 1960," in "Original and Essential Letters," Nelson Papers; "Address to the Princeton University Chapter of the AAUP, April 11, 1961," pg. 2, folder "Letters from Princeton," Nelson Papers; Hyatt, May 14 chronology in box 20, folder "Lawson Case—Press Releases, Memoranda," in Hyatt Papers, VUSC.
55. "Notes on Conversation with Chancellor Branscomb, May 26, 1960," in "Original and Essential Letters," Nelson Papers; Nelson letter to James Adams, November 6, 1960, pgs. 5–6, folder "Letters from Princeton," Nelson Papers; Foster Chronology, 34–36; Nelson, "Address to the Princeton University Chapter of the AAUP, April 11, 1961," pg. 2, in folder "Letters from Princeton," Nelson Papers. Lawson acknowledged his cooperation with the process of readmission, Lawson interview with Warren, tape 1, transcript pg. 13–14.
56. Nelson in *Christian Century*, August 10, 1960, 924. Branscomb in contrast remembered Nelson interrupting the chancellor's speech with a note demanding a decision for Lawson, and Branscomb found the timeline preposterous since Lawson was unlikely to make a decision over two or three days' time.
57. James Sellers, "Reconstruction from Memory of the Meeting of the Admissions Committee with Chancellor Branscomb, May 30, 1960," in "Original and Essential Letters," Nelson Papers; Foster Chronology, 38; *New York Times*, May 31, 1960; "Addendum to the Chancellor's Report to the Board of Trust of Vanderbilt University," October 7, 1960, pgs. e.-f., in folder 14, box V-29, Stahlman Papers; Branscomb, "The Lawson Episode: The Role of Dean Robert Nelson," pgs. 3–4, in box 29, folder "Harvie Branscomb on James Lawson," Centennial History Project. Grade change information in Nelson letter to James Adams, November 6, 1960, pg. 6, folder "Letters from Princeton," Nelson Papers; and "The Lawson Episode—Twenty Years Later," pg. 3, box 4, folder 34, Branscomb Papers. For an example of support for Branscomb's decision, see the June 7, 1960, memo in box 3, folder "Lawson Case," Swint Papers, VUSC.
58. Foster chronology 39–43, 45; Judaic law quotation in Nelson letter to James Adams, November 6, 1960, folder "Letters from Princeton," pg. 7, Nelson Papers. See also *New York Times*, June 1 and June 4, 1960; *Tennessean*, June 2, 1960; *Nashville Banner*, June 3, 1960; *Jet*, June 16, 1960; note that the opinion about Nelson is contradicted in Johnson et al., "The Lawson Affair," 147–48, 162.
59. Nelson quotation in letter to James Adams, November 6, 1960, pg. 7, folder "Letters from Princeton," Nelson Papers; Foster Chronology, 39–43, 45. See also *New York Times*, June 2 and June 4, June 6, 1960; *Tennessean*, June 2, 1960; *Nashville Banner*, June 3, 1960; *Jet*, June 16, 1960; Johnson et al., "The Lawson Affair," 147, 162.

Chapter 3

1. Foster Chronology, 46–53.
2. Nelson to James Adams, November 6, 1960, pgs. 7–8, folder "Letters from Princeton," Nelson Papers; Foster Chronology, 46–56. On Harrelson, see Conkin, *Gone with the Ivy*, 562; *Newsweek*, June 13, 1960, 62.

3. Foster Chronology, 54, 56.
4. Foster Chronology, 56–58; *Newsweek*, June 13, 1960, 62.
5. Nelson to James Adams, November 6, 1960, pg. 8, folder "Letters from Princeton," Nelson Papers; Johnson et al., "The Lawson Affair," 150; Foster Chronology, 56–61; Nelson in *Christian Century*, August 10, 1960, 924.
6. Finishing school anecdote in Johnson et al., "The Lawson Affair," 150–51.
7. Nelson in *Christian Century*, August 10, 1960, 925; Foster Chronology, 65–66.
8. *New York Herald Tribune*, June 6, 1960; Foster Chronology, 65–69; Nelson letter to James Adams, November 6, 1960, pgs. 9–10, folder "Letters from Princeton," Nelson Papers; Silberman, Report at AAUP meeting, June 8, 1960, folder "Original and Essential Letters," Nelson Papers; Johnson et al., "The Lawson Affair," 150–52; letter to Everett Tilson from Jane H. Park (Vanderbilt Medical School), May 1, 1960, in Everett Tilson File, Nashville Room; Johnson et al., "The Lawson Affair," 157. Tilson, "Ugly Rebel," 89; research funding detail in Johnson et al., "The Lawson Affair," 150.
9. Roos in Johnson et al., "The Lawson Affair," 152.
10. Johnson et al., "The Lawson Affair," 151–54; Roos interview by Kathy Bennett, May 19, 2004, Oral History Project, NPL.
11. Johnson et al., "The Lawson Affair," 155–57.
12. Roos, "Forty-Eight Hours at Vanderbilt," Roos Papers, VUSC; Nelson letter to James Adams, November 6, 1960, pgs. 9–10, folder "Letters from Princeton," Nelson Papers; Johnson et al., "The Lawson Affair," 155–58; Foster Chronology, 69–71.
13. Johnson et al., "The Lawson Affair," 155–56.
14. *Tennessean*, June 10, 1960; *New York Times*, June 12, 1960.
15. Roos in Johnson et al., "The Lawson Affair," 159. Petition numbers in Foster Chronology, 76; the 161 signees were out of 195 contacted and 428 total faculty members at Vanderbilt at the time. Nelson letter to James Adams, November 6, 1960, pgs. 9–10, folder "Letters from Princeton," Nelson Papers; Foster Chronology, 71–78; quotation in *Tennessean*, June 10, 1960; Johnson et al., "The Lawson Affair," 151–52, 159–61; *New York Times*, June 11, June 12, 1960; Vanderbilt heart trouble in *Tennessean*, June 13, 1960.
16. Nelson letter to James Adams, November 6, 1960, pgs. 9, 10, folder "Letters from Princeton," Nelson Papers; Foster Chronology, 60; *Tennessean*, June 10, 1960; Silberman, report at AAUP meeting, June 8, 1960, folder "Original and Essential Letters," Nelson Papers. Note also the June 8, 1960, letter to Branscomb from Vanderbilt chemistry professor Larry C. Hall, who noted that both sides agreed on everything except the matter of readmittance—he suggested the university readmit Lawson and follow the Beach Committee protocols accordingly to embed the regulations in university norms, in box 1, folder 2, Nelson Fuson Papers, VUSC.
17. Stahlman's position was pieced together from the following: the two letters (both dated June 11, 1960) to Gertrude and Harold S. Vanderbilt, respectively, in folder "Lawson/Stahlman," box 29, Centennial History Project; memo, June 13, 1960, in box V-19, folder 22, Stahlman Papers, VUSC; letter to Branscomb, June 17, 1960, and letter to J. P. Norfleet, June 20, 1960, both in box 29, folder "Divinity School—Students—Lawson," Centennial History Project. See also Conkin, *Gone with the Ivy*, 566.

18. *New York Times*, June 12, June 14, 1960; Foster Chronology, 78–81.
19. *New York Times*, June 12, June 14, 1960; Nelson letter to James Adams, November 6, 1960, pgs. 10–11, folder "Letters from Princeton," Nelson Papers; Foster Chronology, 78–81; Johnson et al., "The Lawson Affair," 160 (Roos quotation), 166; Conkin, *Gone with the Ivy*, 567–70.
20. Foster Chronology, 83.
21. Foster Chronology, 81–91; *Nashville Banner*, June 16, 1960; *Tennessean*, June 16 ("unjust and ungracious"), and June 17, 1960; *New York Times*, June 15, June 16, June 18, July 27, 1960; *Christian Century*, June 15, 1960, 716; Johnson et al., "The Lawson Affair," 163; Nelson, *Christian Century*, August 10, 925. See also the letters to the editor in *British Weekly*, March 30, 1961, in Everett Tilson File, Nashville Room.
22. First quotation in letter from William Edwards, May 31, 1960, second quotation in letter from White Hall Morrison to Nelson, June 1, 1960, both in folder "Letters of Dissent," Nelson Papers. See also letter from Sam Fleming, June 8, 1960, and response from Nelson, June 10, 1960, both in folder "Original and Essential Letters," Nelson Papers. For an example of the more principled support for Branscomb, see the letter from R. L. Garner (Board of Trust member), May 2, 1960, in box 29, folder "Divinity School Students—Lawson," Centennial History Project.
23. *Nashville News Star*, June 26, 1960 (editorial); Foster Chronology, 92–95; Johnson et al., "The Lawson Affair," 163. Tilson's summary of events appeared in the *British Weekly*, September 1, 1960, copy in Everett Tilson File, Nashville Room.
24. Foster Chronology, 85–86, 89–100; *Time*, June 13, 1960, 59; *Newsweek*, June 13, 1960, 62; *Tennessean*, June 14, 1960; *Nashville News Star*, June 26, 1960; dispatch, June 17, 1960, box 21, folder 415, Dispatches from *Time*; Lawson interview by Warren, tape 1, transcript pg. 16; Tilson interview, Oral History Project, NPL. On the Beach Committee changes, see *Nashville Banner*, June 3, 1960; Conkin, *Gone with the Ivy*, 555.
25. On the endgame leading to Branscomb's statement, see "The Lawson Episode-Twenty Years Later," box 4, folder 34, Branscomb Papers; Stahlman and Ingram dictated memo, June 13, 1960, in box V-19, folder 22, Stahlman Papers. Quotation in Stahlman to Branscomb, June 17, 1960, in box 29, folder "Divinity School Students—Lawson," Centennial History Project; Lovett, *The Civil Rights Movement*, 143.
26. Conkin, *Gone with the Ivy*, 572–74 (and 556 on the Seatlantic Fund requiring open admission for its funding recipients); Branscomb to Ford Foundation in box 29, folder "Chancellor's Files – Lawson," Centennial History Project; Roos, "Forty-Eight Hours at Vanderbilt," Roos Collection, VUSC; Erwin Knoll, "Conflict on the Campus: The Lawson Case at Vanderbilt," *The Progressive*, February 1961, 34–38. See also Nelson to Tilson, January 23, 1961, and letter to Bob and Pat, October 3, 1960, in "Correspondence from Princeton," Nelson Papers, on the Ford Foundation, plus an apparent rumor that Nelson resigned because of his thwarted positioning to succeed Branscomb as chancellor. Roos also noted that the campus rumor was that Nelson would succeed Branscomb. Johnson et al., "The Lawson Affair," 135, and 146 on FOR, plus Roos interview, Oral History Project, NPL. See also the article in *The Washington Post*, August 26, 1960.
27. Conkin, *Gone with the Ivy*, 451; Branscomb, "The Lawson Episode: The Role of Dean Robert Nelson," box 29, folder "Harvie Branscomb on James Lawson," Centennial

History Project, quotations on 1, 4–5, 6; Roos, "Forty-Eight Hours at Vanderbilt," Roos Collection, VUSC.

28. Nelson letter to James Adams, November 6, 1960, pg. 1, folder "Letters from Princeton," Nelson Papers; on Branscomb's hypocrisy, see Nelson letter to W. R. Cole, September 18, 1960, folder "Letters from Princeton," Nelson Papers. Nelson also published a pamphlet, "The Lawson-Vanderbilt Affair: Letters to Dean Nelson," which includes his account of events and letters of support written to him (in box 1, folder 15, Nelson Fuson Papers, VUSC).
29. Nelson to Branscomb, December 25, 1960, in box 4, folder 34, Branscomb Papers; Branscomb to Nelson, May 28, 1963, and Nelson to Branscomb, June 6, 1963, both in folder "Original and Essential Letters," Nelson Papers. See Branscomb's article in *The Christian Century*, April 13, 1960, 454, and Avon Williams's response on April 27, 1960, 517. See also Avon Williams's comments used out of context in Branscomb's "Addendum to the Chancellor's Report to the Board of Trust of Vanderbilt University," October 7, 1960, pgs. i.–j., in box V-29, folder 14, Stahlman Papers.
30. "The Lawson Episode-Twenty Years Later," box 4, folder 34, Branscomb Papers; see also typescript, May 26, 1960, pgs. 12–13, "Chancellor's Files 1–44," box 29, folder "Lawson," Centennial History Project.
31. "Some Comments and Reflections on the Lawson Episode (March - June 1960)," box 29, folder "Branscomb on Lawson," Centennial History Project.
32. This paragraph draws on Everett Tilson's concise eviscerations of Branscomb's position in *Christian Century*, April 27, 1960, and "Ugly Rebel," 15, 18, 24; see also Conkin, *Gone with the Ivy*, 567–70.
33. Conkin, *Gone with the Ivy*, 553, 558; Halberstam, *The Children*, 204.
34. Lawson, *Christian Century*, March 30, 1960, 379; Nelson, "Address to the Princeton University Chapter of the AAUP, April 11, 1961," pg. 3, folder "Letters from Princeton," Nelson Papers. The point on civil authority is made by James L. Adams to Robert Nelson, May 5, 1961, in folder "Letters from Princeton," Nelson Papers. Kean, *Desegregating Higher Education*, 295n115; Conkin, *Gone with the Ivy*, 565.
35. Sellers essay and Duke contrasts in *Concern: A Biweekly Journal of Social and Political Comment*, March 18, 1960 (published by the National Conference of Methodist Youth), in box 16, folder 7, Highlander Folk School Papers, Tennessee State Library and Archives. See also Special Edition, *Wesley Notes*, March 7, 1960 (published by Nashville Wesley Foundation), box 2, folder "Lawson Case" (2 of 2), Madison Sarratt Papers, VUSC; James E. Sellers, "Love, Justice, and the Non-Violent Movement," *Theology Today* 18, no. 4 (1962): 422–34—and see the discussion of this in Richard Lischer, *The Preacher King: Martin Luther King, Jr. and the Word That Moved America* (New York: Oxford University Press, 1997), 230. On the contrast to Nashville's stance, see the other private Southern universities examined in Kean, *Desegregating Higher Education*; Theodore D. Segal, *Point of Reckoning: The Fight for Racial Justice at Duke University* (Durham, NC: Duke University Press, 2021). See also the student publication of the Divinity School, *Prospectus* (March 1980) devoting its issue to the twentieth anniversary of the Lawson Affair.
36. Quotations in Branscomb, November 15, 1980, "The Lawson Episode—Twenty Years Later," box 4, folder 34, Branscomb Papers.

37. Stahlman to Branscomb, June 17, 1960, and Stahlman to J. P. Norfleet, June 20, 1960, both in box 29, folder "Divinity School Students—Lawson," Centennial History Project; Conkin, *Gone with the Ivy*, 566–69, 294n103 and 294n105; *Nashville Banner* editorial, June 14, 1960; "The Lawson Episode-Twenty Years Later," pg. 3, box 4, folder 34, Branscomb Papers. On West, see Houston, *The Nashville Way*, 127–28.
38. The post-Lawson events are treated by Paul Conkin, *Gone with the Ivy*, 575–80. For an even longer overview see Russell Hamilton, interview with Amy Sturgis, July 28, 1998, in Voices of Vanderbilt Oral History Collection, https://diglib.library.vanderbilt.edu/voices-processquery.pl?SID=20250721937413424&code=voices&relator=Russell+Hamilton&general=&submit=Retrieve+Transcripts; Branscomb quotation recounted in Roos, "Forty-Eight Hours at Vanderbilt," Roos Collection, VUSC.
39. Conkin, *Gone with the Ivy*, 643–46. See also Theodore Cross and Robert Bruce Slater, "Michael Eric Dyson and the Vanderbilt Snub: Searching for a 'System Negro,'" *Journal of Blacks in Higher Education*, no. 24 (Summer 1999), 117–19.
40. The fullest account of the apology is in the Joseph Hough interview, Oral History Project, NPL; Hough helped arrange the meeting, as did Will Campbell apparently, per Everett Tilson in his Oral History Project, NPL, interview. See also Conkin, *Gone with the Ivy*, 642–46; Johnson et al., "The Lawson Affair," 161, 165–66, 174–77; Ray Waddle, "Days of Thunder: The Lawson Affair," *Vanderbilt Magazine*, Fall 2002, 38. Note the skepticism and contempt about the apology from Tilson, Oral History Project, NPL, and Beverly Asbury, interviewed by Amy Sturgis, March 7, 1997, Voices of Vanderbilt Oral History Collection, https://diglib.library.vanderbilt.edu/voices-processquery.pl?SID=20250721937413424&codevoices&relator=Beverly+Asbury&general=&submit=Retrieve+Transcripts.
41. Johnson et al., "The Lawson Affair," 161; Ethan Vesely-Flad, *Fellowship Magazine*, June 11, 2024, https://wagingnonviolence.org/forusa/2024/06/remembering-james-lawson-fierce-dedication-power-nonviolent-action; James M. Lawson, *Revolutionary Nonviolence: Organizing for Freedom* (Berkeley: University of California Press, 2024); Kent Wong, Ana Luz González, and James M. Lawson, eds. *Nonviolence and Social Movements: The Teachings of Rev. James M. Lawson Jr.* (Los Angeles: UCLA Center for Labor Research and Education, 2016); James Lawson, "Forty Years Since King: The Memphis Sanitation Strike," *Labor: Studies in Working-Class History of the Americas* 5, no. 1 (2008): 9–13. On Lawson graduating from BU, see *New York Times*, August 21, 1960.
42. Halberstam, *The Children*, 208.

Epilogue

1. On "ambiguity," see Johnson et al., "The Lawson Affair," 162–63.
2. Conkin, *Gone with the Ivy*, 563–64; Sumner, "The Local Press," 167; Johnson et al., "The Lawson Affair," 167, 169, 173; Nelson letter to Adams, November 6, 1960, pg. 11, Nelson Papers.
3. Waddle, "Days of Thunder," 37, 43.

4. Lawson quotation in August Meier, Elliott M. Rudwick, and Francis L. Broderick, *Black Protest Thought in the Twentieth Century*, 2nd ed. (Indianapolis, IN: Bobbs-Merrill, 1971), 310; Divinity faculty member James D. Glasse quoted in *Jet*, June 16, 1960; Waddle, "Days of Thunder," 41; Dallas Blanchard, Oral History Project, NPL; Martin, "The Lawson Affair," 142–65.
5. A good starting point for the rich literature on Southern religion during the civil rights era is Randall J. Stephens, "'It Has to Come from the Hearts of the People': Evangelicals, Fundamentalists, Race, and the 1964 Civil Rights Act," *Journal of American Studies* 50, no. 3 (2016): 559–85.
6. Morgan quotation in dispatch, June 3, 1960, box 21, folder 410, Dispatches from *Time*. See also a postmortem about academic freedom inspired by the Lawson situation in the *Tennessean*, June 19, 1960.
7. Jack Hodgson, "Why Colleges Don't Know What to do About Campus Protests," *Time*, April 29, 2024, https://time.com/6971920/campus-gaza-protests-free-speech-tension; Sharde M. Davis, ed., *Being Black in the Ivory: Truth-Telling About Racism in Higher Education* (Chapel Hill: University of North Carolina Press, 2024); Erin Pineda, *Seeing Like an Activist: Civil Disobedience and the Civil Rights Movement* (New York: Oxford University Press, 2021), 22.
8. Brina Ratangee, "Administration Cancels VSG BDS Amendment Vote, Students Protest," *Vanderbilt Hustler*, March 4, 2024, https://vanderbilthustler.com/2024/03/24/administration-cancels-vsg-bds-amendment-vote-students-protest.
9. Eli Motycka, "Vanderbilt University Arrested Me While I Was Reporting on Student Protests," *Nashville Scene*, March 29, 2024, https://www.nashvillescene.com/news/pithinthewind/eli-motycka-statement-on-vanderbilt-arrest/article_ba7fc6a4-ee12-11ee-831d-ffc2df826dac.html
10. Marianna Bacallao, "What Sets Vanderbilt's Response to Pro-Palestinian Protests Apart from Other Colleges," WPLN, May 9, 2024, https://wpln.org/post/what-sets-vanderbilts-response-to-pro-palestinian-protests-apart-from-other-colleges.
11. Bacallao, "What Sets Vanderbilt's."
12. Daniel Diermeier, "Principled Neutrality," *Inside Higher Ed*, May 04, 2022, https://www.insidehighered.com/views/2022/05/05/academic-leaders-shouldnt-take-political-stances-opinion.
13. Daniel Diermeier, *Reputational Analytics: Public Opinion for Companies* (Chicago: University of Chicago Press, 2023); Tyler Austin Harper, "America's Colleges are Reaping What They Sowed," *The Atlantic*, May 2, 2024, https://www.theatlantic.com/ideas/archive/2024/05/college-activism-hypocrisy/678262.
14. Bacallao, "What Sets Vanderbilt's"; Pineda, *Seeing Like An Activist*, excavates this process more broadly by historicizing and theorizing the concept of civil disobedience—see for example page 24. For a wonderful account about how this memory work plays out in a higher education context, see the intro and coda in Cohen, *Confronting Jim Crow*, and more broadly, Jeanne Theoharis, *A More Beautiful and Terrible History: The Uses and Misuses of Civil Rights History* (Boston: Beacon Press, 2018).
15. Siracusa, *Nonviolence Before King*, 4.
16. Sharfstein, "*Brown*, Massive Resistance," 1,462.

BIBLIOGRAPHY

Manuscript and Archival Collections

Houghton Library, Harvard University
  Dispatches from *Time* Magazine Correspondents Collection

University of Memphis Libraries
  Search for Meaning Committee Papers, Special Collections Department

Nashville Room, Nashville Public Library
  Everett Tilson File
  Nashville Banner Clippings Collection

Wilson Library, University of North Carolina
  Taylor Branch Papers

Tennessee State Library and Archives
  Highlander Folk School Papers
  Jack Knox Papers, 1932–1978, Tennessee Historical Society Collection

Vanderbilt University Special Collections (VUSC)
  Harvie Branscomb Papers
  Centennial History Project Papers
  Nelson Fuson Papers
  Philip Hyatt Papers
  James M. Lawson Jr. Papers
  Edmund M. Morgan Jr. Papers
  John Robert Nelson Papers
  Charles E. Roos Collection
  Madison Sarratt Papers
  Lou Silberman Papers
  James G. Stahlman Papers
  Henry Lee Swint Papers
  Harold S. Vanderbilt Papers

Oral History Collections

Samuel Proctor Oral History Program, University of Florida

Civil Rights Oral History Project Collection, Civil Rights Room, Special Collections Division, Nashville Public Library

Southern Oral History Program Collection, University of North Carolina

Who Speaks for the Negro?: An Archival Collection, Robert Penn Warren Center for the Humanities, Vanderbilt University

Voices of Vanderbilt Oral History Collection

Eyes on the Prize Interviews, Henry Hampton Collection, Washington University Libraries Film and Media Archive

---

Books, Scholarly Articles, and Other Works

Ackerman, Peter, and Jack Duvall. *A Force More Powerful: A Century of Nonviolent Conflict*. New York: St. Martin's, 2000.

Ballantyne, Katherine J. *Radical Volunteers: Dissent, Desegregation, and Student Power in Tennessee*. Athens: University of Georgia Press, 2024.

Berry, Keith W. "Charles S. Johnson, Fisk University, and the Struggle for Civil Rights, 1945–1970." PhD diss., Florida State University, 2005.

Bingham, Emily, and Thomas A. Underwood, eds., *The Southern Agrarians and the New Deal: Essays After I'll Take My Stand*. Charlottesville: University of Virginia Press, 2001.

Branch, Taylor. *Parting the Waters, America in the King Years, 1965–1963*. New York: Simon & Schuster, 2007.

Bromley, Dorothy Dunbar, and Susan McCabe, "Impact of the Sit-in Movement on Academic Freedom." *Negro Educational Review* 12, no. 2 (April 1, 1961).

Burnam, Paul. "Everett Tilson: Pioneer in the Condemnation of White Privilege." *Ohio History* 127, no. 1 (Spring 2020), 87–103.

Byrd, James P., Jr. "Charting a New Vision: The School of Religion." In *Vanderbilt Divinity School: Education, Contest, and Change*, edited by Dale A. Johnson. Nashville, TN: Vanderbilt University Press, 2001.

Carey, Bill. *Chancellors, Commodores and Coeds: A History of Vanderbilt University*. Nashville, TN: Clearbook Press, 2003.

Cline, David P. *From Reconciliation to Revolution: The Student Interracial Ministry, Liberal Christianity, and the Civil Rights Movement*. Chapel Hill: University of North Carolina Press, 2016.

Coffman, Elesha J. *The Christian Century and the Rise of the Protestant Mainline*. New York: Oxford University Press, 2013.

Cohen, Robert. *Confronting Jim Crow: Race, Memory, and the University of Georgia in the Twentieth Century*. Chapel Hill: University of North Carolina Press, 2024.

Cole, Eddie R. *The Campus Color Line: College Presidents and the Struggle for Black Freedom.* Princeton, NJ: Princeton University Press, 2020.

Conkin, Paul K. *Gone With the Ivy: A Biography of Vanderbilt University.* Knoxville: University of Tennessee, 1985.

Conkin, Paul K. *The Southern Agrarians.* Knoxville: University of Tennessee Press, 1988.

Cornfield, Daniel B., Jonathan S. Coley, Larry W. Isaac, and Dennis C. Dickerson. "The Making of a Movement: An Intergenerational Mobilization Model of the Nonviolent Nashville Civil Rights Movement." *Social Science History* 45, no. 3 (2021): 469–94.

Cross, Theodore, and Robert Bruce Slater, "Michael Eric Dyson and the Vanderbilt Snub: Searching for a 'System Negro.'" *Journal of Blacks in Higher Education*, no. 24 (Summer 1999): 117–19.

Davis, Sharde M., ed. *Being Black in the Ivory: Truth-Telling About Racism in Higher Education.* Chapel Hill: University of North Carolina Press, 2024.

Day, Jonathan. "A Breech in the Wall: The Vanderbilt University Student Community and the 1960s." BA thesis, Vanderbilt University, 1996.

Dickerson, Dennis C. "James M. Lawson, Jr.: Methodism, Nonviolence and the Civil Rights Movement." *Methodist History* 52, no. 3 (April 2014): 168–87.

Dickerson, Dennis C. "Humanity Defined, Hypocrisy Defied: Sacralizing the Black Freedom Struggle, 1930–60." *Studies in Church History*, no. 60 (2024): 477–510.

Diermeier, Daniel. *Reputational Analytics: Public Opinion for Companies.* Chicago: University of Chicago Press. 2023.

Doyle, Don H. *Nashville Since the 1920s.* Knoxville: University of Tennessee Press, 1985.

Eagles, Charles W. "The Closing of Mississippi Society: Will Campbell, 'The $64,000 Question,' and Religious Emphasis Week at the University of Mississippi." *Journal of Southern History* 67, no. 2 (2001): 331–72.

Egerton, John. *Speak Now Against the Day: The Generation Before the Civil Rights Movement in the South.* Chapel Hill: University of North Carolina Press, 1994.

Fleming, Cynthia Griggs. "C. T. Vivian: Disciple of Assertive Nonviolence." *AME Church Review* 118, no. 387 (July–September 2002): 26–54.

Foster, Susan Leigh. "Choreographies of Protest." *Theatre Journal* 55, no. 3 (2003): 395–412.

Franklin, V. P. *The Young Crusaders: The Untold Story of the Children and Teenagers Who Galvanized the Civil Rights Movement.* New York: Beacon Press, 2021.

Gilmore, Glenda Elizabeth. *Defying Dixie: The Radical Roots of Civil Rights, 1919–1950.* New York: W.W. Norton, 2008.

Graham, Hugh Davis. *Crisis in Print: Desegregation and the Press in Tennessee.* Nashville, TN: Vanderbilt University Press, 1967.

Halberstam, David. *The Children.* New York: Random House, 1998.

Harris, Paul William. *A Long Reconstruction: Racial Caste and Reconciliation in the Methodist Episcopal Church.* New York: Oxford University Press, 2022.

Harvey, Paul. *Freedom's Coming: Religious Culture and the Shaping of the South from the Civil War Through the Civil Rights Era.* Chapel Hill: University of North Carolina Press Books, 2005.

Hawkins, Merrill M. *Will Campbell: Radical Prophet of the South.* Macon, GA: Mercer University Press, 1997.

Haynes, Stephen R. *The Last Segregated Hour: The Memphis Kneel-ins and the Campaign for Southern Church Desegregation.* New York: Oxford University Press, 2012.

Hogan, Wesley C. *Many Minds, One Heart: SNCC's Dream for a New America.* Chapel Hill: University of North Carolina Press, 2007.

Hoover, Judith. "The Nashville Sit-Ins: Successful Nonviolent Direct Action through Rhetorical Invention and Advocacy." In *Like Wildfire: The Rhetoric of the Civil Rights Sit-Ins*, edited by Sean Patrick O'Rourke and Lesli K. Pace. Columbia: University of South Carolina Press, 2020.

Houston, Benjamin. *The Nashville Way: Racial Etiquette and the Struggle for Social Justice in a Southern City.* Athens: University of Georgia Press, 2012.

Houston, Benjamin. "The Aquinas of the Rednecks: Reconciliation, the Southern Character, and the Bootleg Ministry of Will D. Campbell." *Sixties: A Journal of History, Politics, and Culture* 4, no. 2 (December 2011): 135–50.

Houston, Benjamin. "Donald Davidson and the Segregationist Intellect." In *Southern Character: Essays in Honor of Bertram Wyatt-Brown*, edited by Lisa Tendrich Frank and Daniel Kilbride. Gainesville: University Press of Florida, 2011.

Isaac, Larry W., Daniel B. Cornfield, Dennis C. Dickerson, James M. Lawson, and Jonathan S. Coley, "'Movement Schools' and Dialogical Diffusion of Nonviolent Praxis: Nashville Workshops in the Southern Civil Rights Movement." In *Nonviolent Conflict and Civil Resistance*, edited by Sharon Erickson Nepstead, and Lester R. Kurtz. Leeds, UK: Emerald Publishing, 2012.

Johnson, Dale A., ed. *Vanderbilt Divinity School: Education, Contest, and Change.* Nashville, TN: Vanderbilt University Press, 2001.

Johnson, Dale A., James M. Lawson, Gene L. Davenport, Langdon Gilkey, Lou H. Silberman, John Compton, and Charles Roos. "The Lawson Affair, 1960: A Conversation." In *Vanderbilt Divinity School: Education, Contest, and Change*, ed. Dale A. Johnson. Nashville, TN: Vanderbilt University Press, 2001.

Kapur, Sudarshan. *Raising Up a Prophet: The African-American Encounter with Gandhi.* Boston: Beacon Press, 1992.

Kean, Melissa. *Desegregating Private Higher Education in the South: Duke, Emory, Rice, Tulane and Vanderbilt.* Baton Rouge: Louisiana State University Press, 2008.

Kean, Melissa. "The Early, Unsuccessful Effort to Desegregate Duke University." *Journal of Blacks in Higher Education*, no. 62 (2008): 84–86.

Kendi, Ibram X. *The Black Campus Movement: Black Students and the Racial Reconstitution of Higher Education, 1965–1972.* New York: Springer, 2012.

King, Mary E. *Freedom Song: A Personal Story of the 1960s Civil Rights Movement.* New York: Morrow, 1987.

Kneebone, John T. *Southern Liberal Journalists and the Issue of Race, 1920–1944.* Chapel Hill: University of North Carolina Press, 1985.

Kosek, Joseph Kip. "Religion and Nonviolence in American History." *Religion Compass*, no. 6 (2012), 402–13.

Kuryla, Peter A. "James Lawson, Jr., and the 1968 Memphis Sanitation Workers' Strike." *AME Church Review*, July–September 2002, 57.

Lawson, James M. "Forty Years Since King: The Memphis Sanitation Strike." *Labor: Studies in Working-Class History of the Americas* 5, no. 1 (2008): 9–13.

Lawson, James M., Jr. *Revolutionary Nonviolence: Organizing for Freedom.* Berkeley: University of California Press, 2024.

Lewis, George. *Massive Resistance: The White Response to the Civil Rights Movement.* London: Bloomsbury Academic, 2006.

Limbo, Ernest M. "James Lawson: The Nashville Civil Rights Movement." In *The Human Tradition in the Civil Rights Movement*, edited by Susan Glisson. Lanham, MD: Rowman & Littlefield, 2006.

Lischer, Richard. *The Preacher King: Martin Luther King, Jr. and the Word that Moved America.* New York: Oxford University Press, 1997.

Lovett, Bobby L. *The Civil Rights Movement in Tennessee: A Narrative History.* Knoxville: University of Tennessee Press, 2005.

Martin, A. W. "The Lawson Affair, the Sit-Ins, and Beyond: Observations of an Eyewitness." *Tennessee Historical Quarterly* 75, no. 2 (2016): 142–65.

McDuffie, Scott Patterson. "James Lawson: Leading Architect and Educator of Nonviolence and Nonviolent Direct Action Protest Strategies During the Student Sit-in Movement of 1960." MA thesis, North Carolina State University, 2007.

Meier, August, Elliott M. Rudwick, and Francis L Broderick, eds. *Black Protest Thought in the Twentieth Century*, 2nd ed. Indianapolis: Bobbs-Merrill, 1971.

Michel, Gregg L. *Struggle for a Better South: The Southern Student Organizing Committee, 1964–1969.* New York: Palgrave Macmillan, 2004.

Michel, Gregg L. *Spying on Students: The FBI, Red Squads, and Student Activists in the 1960s South.* Baton Rouge: Louisiana State University Press, 2024.

Morgan, Iwan, and Philip Davies, eds. *From Sit-Ins to SNCC: The Student Civil Rights Movements in the 1960s.* Gainesville: University Press of Florida, 2012.

Morris, Aldon D. *The Origins of the Civil Rights Movement.* New York: Simon and Schuster, 1984.

Murphy, Paul V. *The Rebuke of History: The Southern Agrarians and American Conservative Thought.* Chapel Hill: University of North Carolina Press, 2003.

Murphy, Paul V. "The Social Memory of the South: Donald Davidson and the Tennessee Past." *Tennessee Historical Quarterly* 55, no. 3 (Fall 1996): 257–69.

Murray, Peter C. *Methodists and the Crucible of Race, 1930–1975.* Columbia: University of Missouri Press, 2004.

Oppenheimer, Martin. *The Sit-in Movement of 1960.* Brooklyn: Carlson, 1989.

Paris, Peter J. "The African American Presence in the Divinity School." In *Vanderbilt Divinity School: Education, Contest, and Change*, edited by Dale A. Johnson. Nashville, TN: Vanderbilt University Press, 2001.

Phillips, Betsy. *Dynamite Nashville: Unmasking the FBI, the KKK, and the Bombers Beyond Their Control.* Nashville, TN: Third Man Books, 2024.

Pineda, Erin R. *Seeing Like an Activist: Civil Disobedience and the Civil Rights Movement.* New York: Oxford University Press, 2021.

Plumley, Byron L., Jr. "Searching for a Place To Stand: Reflections of Spiritually Rooted Social Activists." PhD diss., Union Institute, 1993.

Robbins, Richard. *Sidelines Activist: Charles S. Johnson and the Struggle for Civil Rights.* Jackson: University Press of Mississippi, 1996.

Royals, Tom. *Conversations with Will D. Campbell.* Jackson: University of Mississippi Press, 2018.

Sanders-Cassell, Katrina Marie. *Intelligent and Effective Direction: The Fisk University Race Relations Institute and the Struggle for Civil Rights, 1944–1969.* New York: Peter Lang, 2005.

Sarvis, Will. "Leaders in the Court and Community: Z. Alexander Looby, Avon N. Williams, Jr., and the Legal Fight for Civil Rights in Tennessee, 1940–1970." *Journal of African American History* 88, no. 1 (2003): 42–58.

Schmidt, Christopher W. *The Sit-Ins: Protest and Legal Change in the Civil Rights Era.* Chicago: University of Chicago Press, 2019.

Segal, Theodore D. *Point of Reckoning: The Fight for Racial Justice at Duke University.* Durham, NC: Duke University Press, 2021.

Sharfstein, Daniel J. "*Brown*, Massive Resistance, and the Lawyer's View: A Nashville Story." *Vanderbilt Law Review* 74, no. 5 (October 2021): 1,435–66.

Shattuck, Gardiner H., Jr. *Episcopalians and Race: Civil War to Civil Rights.* Lexington: University Press of Kentucky, 2014.

Silk, Mark. *Spiritual Politics: Religion and America Since World War II.* New York: Simon and Schuster, 1989.

Siracusa, Anthony C. *Nonviolence Before King: The Politics of Being and the Black Freedom Struggle.* Chapel Hill: University of North Carolina Press, 2021.

Siracusa, Anthony C. "Understanding Militant Non-violence Within Memphis' Modern Civil Rights Movement: The Leadership and Witness of the Rev. James M. Lawson Jr." Memphis: Rhodes College Institute for Regional Studies, 2007.

Siracusa, Anthony C. "From Pacifism to Resistance: The Evolution of Nonviolence in Wartime America." *Journal of Civil and Human Rights* 3, no. 1 (Spring/Summer 2017): 57–77.

Siracusa, Anthony C. "'The Doctrine of Truth's Many Sides': Jain Religion, James Lawson, and the Politics of Nonviolence in the Black Freedom Struggle." *West Tennessee Historical Society Papers*, no. 70 (2016), 21–36.

Siracusa, Anthony C. "Building the Most Durable Weapon: Rethinking The Origins of Non-Violence in the U.S. Struggle for Civil Rights." MA thesis, Vanderbilt University, 2015.

Siracusa, Anthony C. "Developing an American Ahimsa: The Rev. James M. Lawson Jr.'s Paradigm of Protest." BA thesis, Rhodes College, 2009.

Slate, Nico. *Colored Cosmopolitanism: The Shared Struggle for Freedom in the United States and India.* Cambridge, MA: Harvard University Press, 2012.

Slate, Nico. "The Drama of Nonviolence: Theatre as Education Within the American Civil Rights Movement." *Research in Drama Education* 27, no. 1 (2022): 73–87.

Sosna, Morton. *In Search of the Silent South: Southern Liberals and the Race Issue*. New York: Columbia University Press, 1977.

Stephens, Randall J. "'It Has to Come from the Hearts of the People': Evangelicals, Fundamentalists, Race, and the 1964 Civil Rights Act." *Journal of American Studies* 50, no. 3 (2016): 559–85.

Sumner, David E. "The Local Press and the Nashville Student Movement, 1960." PhD diss., University of Tennessee, 1989.

Sumner, David E. "The Publisher and the Preacher: Racial Conflict at Vanderbilt University." *Tennessee Historical Quarterly* 56, no. 1 (1997), 34–43.

Theoharis, Jeanne. *A More Beautiful and Terrible History: The Uses and Misuses of Civil Rights History*. Boston: Beacon Press, 2018.

Turner, Jeffrey A. *Sitting In and Speaking Out: Student Movements in the American South, 1960–1970*. Athens: University of Georgia Press, 2010.

Vivian, C. T., and Steve Fiffer. *It's in the Action: Memories of a Nonviolent Warrior*. Montgomery, AL: NewSouth Books, 2021.

Waddle, Ray. "Days of Thunder: The Lawson Affair." *Vanderbilt Magazine*, Fall 2002, 34–43.

Wallenstein, Peter, ed. *Higher Education and the Civil Rights Movement: White Supremacy, Black Southerners, and College Campuses*. Gainesville: University Press of Florida, 2008.

Wechsler, Harold S., and Steven J. Diner. *Unwelcome Guests: A History of Access to American Higher Education*. Baltimore, MD: Johns Hopkins University Press, 2021.

Williamson-Lott, Joy Ann. *Jim Crow Campus: Higher Education and the Struggle for a New Southern Social Order*. New York: Teachers College Press, 2018.

Williamson-Lott, Joy Ann. "The Battle Over Power, Control, and Academic Freedom at Southern Institutions of Higher Education, 1955–1965." *Journal of Southern History* 79, no. 4 (November 2013): 879–920.

Winchell, Mark Royden. *Where No Flag Flies: Donald Davidson and the Southern Resistance*. Columbia: University of Missouri Press, 2000.

Wolcott, Victoria W. *Living in the Future: Utopianism and the Long Civil Rights Movement*. Chicago: University of Chicago Press, 2022.

Wong, Kent, Ana Luz González, and James M. Lawson Jr., eds. *Nonviolence and Social Movements: The Teachings of Rev. James M. Lawson Jr.* Los Angeles: UCLA Center for Labor Research and Education, 2016.

Wynn, Linda T. "The Dawning of a New Day: The Nashville Sit-Ins, February 13–May 10, 1960." *Tennessee Historical Quarterly* 50, no. 1 (1991): 42–54.